Not So Private Lives

Alan Shelley

authorHOUSE®

AuthorHouse™ UK Ltd.
500 Avebury Boulevard
Central Milton Keynes, MK9 2BE
www.authorhouse.co.uk
Phone: 08001974150

Permission to reproduce extracts from Noel Coward's Private Lives
has been granted by Methuen Drama, an imprint of A&C Black.

Extracts from the songs I Went To A Marvelous Party, Someday I'll Find
You, The Stately Homes Of England and Sail Away reproduced by kind
permission of Alan Brodie Representation Ltd (abr@alanbrodie.com) on behalf
of NC Aventales AG, successor in title to the Estate of Noel Coward.

First published by AuthorHouse 7/7/2009

ISBN: 978-1-4389-8415-5 (sc)

This book is printed on acid-free paper.

For Maia and Rachel

and

The Festival Players

AMANDA: I think very few people are completely normal really, deep down in their private lives. It all depends on a combination of circumstances. If all the various cosmic thingummys fuse at the same moment, and the right spark is struck, there's no knowing what one mightn't do. That was the trouble with Elyot and me, we were like two violent acids bubbling about in a nasty little matrimonial bottle.

Private Lives

Chapter One

The Autumn Choice

I SUGGESTED *Who's Afraid of Virginia Woolf* but no one listens to me, not even when I am sitting behind a curtain back-stage acting as the prompt. More often than not I am also ignored when they choose the lucky person to be accorded that honour; my usual role is helping with the props or sewing on sequins. Nevertheless, I am a member of the Committee because no one else in the Great Selsdon Amateur Dramatic Society is prepared to take on the job of Secretary. As most of you will know, with organisations of this kind the Secretary does most of the work and gets only the faintest whiff of recognition, but there is one advantage that comes with this thankless role; I am privy to what goes on. Well, most of what goes on. Happenings behind closed doors need to be conjectured, unless I am the one the 'happening' is happening to, but my extensive knowledge of the participators in the great game of 'what is going on' means that my surmises are often fairly accurate. Please do not get the wrong impression. I am not a spy or a voyeur and I am too diffident to be a purveyor of salacious gossip. I am a reporter: I am a camera. Not to be confused with the 1951 play of that name by John Van Druten that inspired the musical *Cabaret*. We did *Bell, Book and Candle* a few years ago but otherwise Mr Van Druten's name is rarely mentioned at our meetings these days and we do not do musicals; well not very often. I prepare the minutes as a true record of what is discussed and then, for my own pleasure, I document the minutiae of what takes place during the Society's productions although, as you will observe, I became rather more involved with the flotsam and jetsam of this autumn's spectacular than is normally the case.

Trevor rattles on. He has been the Chairman for as long as anyone can remember. There was an attempted coup d'etat three years ago but the least said about that the better. Perhaps I should add a footnote to that remark. Phrases like, 'least said, soonest mended' only whet the appetite as to why the event in question should be the 'least' talked about. Of course, you could interpret my use of this phrase as reluctance on my part to revisit the past. Old wounds, perhaps. Well, I was involved in a minor but inconsequential way behind the scenes, but as the coup leader was more concerned with a feminist agenda than any serious attempt to unseat the incumbent chairman, it was doomed to failure from the start.

Helen chose the wrong General. She did briefly discuss this campaign with me before the first shot was fired but after rejecting her own husband, my candidate, and settling for the Reverend Bob, there was little more I could do. Our Vicar believes in the equality of the sexes but when, as an opening gambit, he suggested that as lady members were in the majority one of them should be considered as Chairman, he was heading for defeat before he had left the trenches. The name of a prospective Chairwoman was never uttered but phrases such as 'needs a male captain to steer this difficult vessel' or 'grasp of financial affairs' or 'superior masculine logic' erupted spontaneously from two or three of those around the table who wear collars and ties. Financial affairs; what a joke. Jackson Tollemache, who works in the Finance Department at the Council, is supposed to be the Treasurer but you can guess who prepares the end of year accounts and monitors the bank statements.

I would have been delighted to see a woman chairing the Society, particularly if it was the efficient, no-nonsense Helen Thurston Brown: with a female in charge I might get a little more recognition for my sterling contribution. I was therefore resolved to champion this cause but easier said than done. Direct intervention by me into the debate, if the Vicar's feeble efforts could be so described, would have been very counter-productive indeed; a comment by our little Secretary would only confirm the male imperative, but I did spend some time with that particular man of the cloth attempting to mastermind his campaign, with an outstandingly disappointing result. I said Helen chose the wrong general, but he was, poor dear, the most lost of all causes. As my mother would say, "Couldn't organise a 'something' in a brewery." How did he produce all those children?

Whatever, the Vicar said no more and Helen diverted her energies towards setting up a more militant feminist splinter group within the Women's Institute.

When Trevor paused for breath, Roger joined the opposition to Albee's play. Obviously does not fancy himself as George. There was some minor support from Tricia who, amazingly, seemed to covet the role of Martha but that did not progress my cause, if that is what it was. Her forte is the part of the maid, or the somnolent Grandmother who sits in virtual silence throughout the play in one corner of the kitchen, and not a neurotic New Englander. I suppose she had seen Elizabeth Taylor in the film, which makes her ambition even more absurd.

No member of the Committee had ambitions to play the young couple. It is not a young committee. Not an unusual situation; we are always short of young people which makes it even more surprising that I am so ignored. I am one of the most attractive under thirty females in the Group, at least that is my view, but my good looks and genuine interest in the Society do not compensate for the apparently incurable disease I am infected with: a virulent strain of stage-fright.

Some people have a fear of heights, others of confined spaces or then there are spiders. With Winston Smith it was rats. Phobias difficult to overcome, but mine seems equally untreatable. However much I try to reason with myself I become tongue tied if I am on stage, even if there is only one person in the audience. I have tried reciting lines to a completely empty auditorium: there was some improvement but I still felt my blood pressure rising and then my eyes began to water so I could not see the script, or the empty hall. There is a famous passage by Mark Twain on the subject.

I recall the occasion of my first appearance.... I got to the theatre forty-five minutes before the hour set for the lecture. My knees were shaking so that I didn't know whether I could stand up. If there is an awful, horrible malady in the world, it is stage-fright – and seasickness. They are a pair. I had stage-fright then for the first and last time. I was only sea-sick once, too. It was on a little ship on which there were two hundred other passengers. I – was – sick. I was so sick there wasn't any left for the other passengers.

I have never been on a ship in rough weather so I cannot confirm or deny his contention, but I do know something about shaking knees. Part of the reason is that I take after my father, and not my mother, so I am naturally of a retiring disposition although I like people and most times am able to conduct an intelligent conversation with them; but one whiff of the greasepaint and I am a trembling wreck. So, you ask, why am I a member of an amateur dramatic society – an organisation that stages plays for public performance requiring thespians to speak out to a room full of spectators – a horde of strangers – who have paid good money to hear the words written by the playwright, emoted in confident and engaging tones by the actors? Well, I will tell you.

I have read of the extraordinarily camaraderie that developed in the trenches during World War One. Men thrown together in close proximity to each other and suffering the most appalling conditions become as close as if they had been married for fifty years. Perhaps not an apt comparison. I have known of husbands and wives who have been together for decades with very little comradeship in their lives, but I think you know to what I am alluding. The same bonding may occur in boarding schools, I cannot say, but that extraordinary phenomenon bred in the mud of Flanders is well documented and even the most excessive of Wackford Squeers can hardly be compared to the threat of the Hun and the conditions of those trenches. Well, I find a similar situation, an equal irrational bonding, within members of societies like ours.

I have no knowledge of sister organisations, but I suspect we are all the same. It is a form of obsessive behaviour. The usual hard-core enter a new campaign with enthusiasm, even fervour, and then after a few drinks at the last night party join in the chorus of, 'Thank God that is over. Never again.' The most hardened members join in the chorus but are also heard to retort that their fellow sufferers intoned the same refrain last time but are here once again, to which all and sundry attest that they mean it this time. They do not. A few weeks go by, and the fever attacks again.

"John. Can I put you down for front of house, and presumably you will help with the set as usual. Now, who's up for props?"

"Where are we to find a biddable cat?"

"We do not want him doing Higgins again."

"Another one. So soon. OK, I'm game."

You might imagine this perverse enthusiasm is strongest in those who will be on stage burnishing their egos and amazing their friends and family as they become, for four nights only, funny or glamorous or tragical or heroic. That is so; but the foot soldiers of the group are equally unable to resist the call of 'show business'.

Everything about it is appealing.....
The costumes, the scen'ry, the makeup, the props.
The audience that lifts you when you're down.

I paint an idealistic picture. Some folk join because they are lonely and it gives them something to do on dark winter evenings or they like the idea of being involved in 'a spot of culture'. Others turn up because their spouse has a leading role on the stage proper and they want to be there in the wings to applaud their efforts – or see they do not stray into the arms of their fictional lovers – but, I maintain, most of us are in the grip of this fever because we are addicted. We cannot control ourselves. It is ridiculous. Mind you, there are one or two of our members that I think should be admitted to a specialist clinic where they might be persuaded to kick the habit. The Scotlands perhaps.

The only other member of the Committee who speaks out and provides some counter-balance to Trevor is Ambrose Percy, our usual Director – or Producer if you like: some amateur theatre companies prefer the latter title. They are quite a double act, Trevor and Ambrose, as they follow some tradition in this field whereby neither listens to the other.

There are rich precedents for this behaviour. Gracie Allen may have listened to her husband, George Burns, but understood little of what he said while in the case of Abbott and Costello, Lou hears what Bud says but is tricked into total confusion by the straight man. The others; the comic who ignores his foil; the politician who only provides an answer to a question by asking one of his own; elderly folk who meet every day as great friends whose conversation is littered with people unknown to the listener, who in any case is not listening but providing a similar catalogue of strangers. In the case of Trevor and Ambrose the subject is common to both of them but they steer their own course through this sea of confused dialogue.

"Our audiences want something light. Something to laugh at in these hard times. A farce to cheer us all up."

"We should concentrate on light comedy. Life is depressing enough as it is. Feydeau perhaps."

"They don't want anything too difficult."

"Keep it simple."

"Should we have another go at *Pygmalion*?"

"Not that they're all bone-headed. A bit of thought-provoking theatre is sometimes called for."

"*No Sex Please, We're British* was one of our big successes."

"Bernard Shaw perhaps? Do we have a Joan amongst us? If a Dorothy can be found, a Maid of Orleans must be out there somewhere? "

"Can't afford a costume drama. Not after last Christmas and that Wizard fiasco."

The Treasure said nothing but I informed all present that at the moment the bank balance was in a healthy state – even robust. The Chairman actually heard what I said.

"We can be ambitious then. *The Rivals*? We have lots of people who can play that woman who gets all the words wrong."

"On the other hand, what about a murder mystery?"

"Or the one about the handbag left on a bus?"

"Nothing that needs a kitchen sink. Or any angry young men."

"Agatha Christie – or *Billy Liar* is fun, but we don't have the youngsters."

"That chap who stays in Blackpool – or is it Scarborough? What's his name? Oh yes, Aykbourn."

"*The Entertainer*? But we don't have anyone that can dance."

"Something romantic, I fancy."

"*No Sex Please, We're British*. Not again. That was awful."

"We haven't done a Rattigan recently."

"We should look at Rattigan again."

At this point they must have heard the repetition of the name Rattigan.

"No, Ambrose, my dear fellow. Not after the disaster with *The Winslow Boy*."

"That wasn't my fault."

"I'm not suggesting you were the father."

"I should hope not. But she was a pretty thing. Is she still around?"

I told them Betty Jackson had moved to Scotland. We had not been able to find a suitable boy to play Ronnie and Betty volunteered to cut her hair short and help us out. She was small and slim but unfortunately she became pregnant before opening night and Trevor wanted to cancel the show. Ambrose had rebelled at that – he rebelled about a lot of things – and insisted we went ahead with an *enceinte* boy. Trevor said it was a scandal; washed his hands of the whole production. Not that that made any difference; he never did anything anyway, except make a speech at the last night party. I say a speech. More accurately it is best termed as 'the speech'. It never varies. In fact, over time, it has became so standard we all listened one night to a flow of accolades being accorded to the splendid cast of *Ring Round the Moon*, one of the plays we had staged the year before.

"Rattigan is a safe bet."

"I think we've seen enough of Mr Rattigan."

"I'm told he's a – you know what."

"We don't go in for that sort of thing here."

"Alternatively, what about Coward?"

"What about the ever dependable Coward? Our dear Noël."

Trevor stressed to the word 'Noël' as if he was about to sing us a Christmas carol but as this thought entered my mind I went on to say to myself, is not Mr C also said to be a 'you know what.' Nevertheless, when the two of them managed to get into a dialogue, rather than a competition, a firm inclination towards *Private Lives* emerged.

At this point the Vicar interrupted the discussion. He stuttered: a severe handicap in his trade, and on the stage, but there he is generally only trusted with a paint brush. In the pulpit he managed somehow. Perhaps like Trevor and his last night speech, the sermons are so familiar to the parishioners that those of them who are awake do not need the words; they have heard them all before. In different combinations perhaps but with a text that varies little. He is not all that much older than me and a member of the Committee because Trevor thinks the Church should be represented. Having made that concession, the Chairman tends to ignore him.

"Mr Chairman. Delightful play, but a difficult s s set. If I remember it is a t t terrace, at a hotel in France, and a f f flat in Paris. Quite a f f feat for the stage at the Church Hall."

"Oh Robert."

It was the Rev Robert Milk, but he had asked everyone to call him Bob. We all did, except for the precious Trevor Jointing JP.

"We can overcome that little problem, surely. You know how ingenious Eric is."

I managed to break in at this point. Eric Winstanley, the local butcher, was invariably landed with the job of Stage Manager. My mother worked in his shop.

"I am told Eric does not want to be the Stage Manager again. He is going to audition for a part. He's bought himself a pink shirt and he's growing a beard."

"A beard. What's that got to do with a terrace in France? I'll have a word with him. Now, all we have to do is make a decision about a Director."

All eyes turned towards Ambrose. He smiled and placed the tips of his fingers together that he saw as a gesture of modesty but I thought it made him look like Uriah Heep. At the same time he closed his eyes for a moment and then nodded his head. None of us were surprised at this outcome. He never did the pantomimes, but other than that it would not have been stretching the bounds of credulity if we had changed our name to *The Ambrose Percy Ensemble* so as to represent the fact that Ambrose is, to all intents and purposes, our Resident Director There might have been some opposition to this situation except that in most amateur groups it is a thankless job, and ours is no exception.

On the professional stage the Director directs the players, and little more, but with people like us the unfortunate incumbent has to ensure that all of the other myriad activities involved in the 'putting on of a play' are in order. The set needs constant supervision to test that it is not going to fall over in mid scene and if the leading man languidly lights a cigarette just after his entrance, the Director will be well advised to check that the cigarette box on the coffee table is not empty. More unfortunate; there are errors in the programme. The leading man's name is incorrectly spelt and reference to the lady who made all the costumes is omitted altogether; Grandma has lost her wig and the femme fatale has chickenpox; or her costume is so poorly stitched that more of her upper body becomes visible during the main love scene than would meet with the Lord Chamberlain's approval. It is not therefore difficult to see why all and sundry are prepared to leave it to Ambrose. If he is prepared to take the responsibility, who are we to complain or mutter about a 'closed' shop – and in any case, he is a very good Director, if you can overlook his sporadic temper tantrums.

The proposal to present *Private Lives* as our autumn show with Ambrose Percy as the Director was approved without any further debate.

I can already envisage a problem with recounting the trials and tribulations associated with this production. There have been trials and tribulations connected to most of our productions but *Private Lives* proved to be a more than classic example. No, the difficulty I see is that not only do I need to describe our members, with all their foibles and fancies, but I have to carefully distinguish between the real-life actors themselves and the characters invented by Mr Coward. I make this point because the amateur actor often becomes so deeply involved in the part they are chosen to play they begin to transmogrify into the fictional character, as I think might have been the case with Roger Scotland.

This phenomenon may occur, in some instances, on the professional stage but within the arena I am familiar with there is at least one case of this experience in most every production. We have never done *Macbeth*, thank goodness, and I am also glad to say there are no plans to stage *Sweeney Todd: The Demon Barber of Fleet Street* with our Gentlemen's Hairdresser in the cast, but I recall an upright and sober headmaster becoming temporarily addicted to the whisky bottle after playing the tutor, Dr Frank Bryant, in *Educating Rita*. Even worse was a read-through we did of *Glengarry Glen Ross* that led to a walk out of negotiators at the local firm of estate agents. It must have struck a strange chord with the Manager who had been at the reading: we never staged it; too avant-garde for us.

I shall, however, try to distinguish fact from fiction in *Private Lives*. This should not be too difficult; Great Selsdon is hardly Peyton Place and can scarcely be compared with the gay Paree inhabited by Coward's characters.

To begin with, let me introduce myself. No one else will ever read these words and so I can be totally honest and candid in all I record. My name is May Twining and I am an attractive woman of around twenty six summers. I work at Lloyds Bank as a cashier, have non-virginal status and am unmarried. I do not want to boast about losing my maidenhead. It came about from an event, some years past, that I do not recall with any pleasure. I think it was the loss of dignity more than the other thing that troubles me the most. As a result of more recent liaisons, I can confirm that Reg was not particularly well endowed but he did have a Morris Minor. The antic we were involved in on the backseat of that car, which he referred to as Matilda – he was the sort of man that gives a name to his automobile – was uncomfortable, unpleasurable and indeed verging on the farcical. I can only bless the fates that decreed he be posted to Southampton before we had time to attempt a repeat of such a pathetic performance. There was no second night for that comic production.

My father died when I was still at school. My recollection is that he was a kindly man who did not say very much: speech is always going to be difficult if the teeth are permanently engaged around a Charatan pipe. Did he, I wonder, remove it when I was conceived? My mother was sad when he died, as of course was I, but she soon recovered; perhaps the absence of the St Bruno aroma was welcome. As I have already said, she works at Winstanley and Son, the butchers in the High Street. She is a happy person; extrovert and content with her life. She plays bingo on Mondays but the highlight of the week is the Saturday night visit to the Bull with a large crowd of friends she has known since school days. Some are married, some are single, some are divorced and one, Heather Robertson, is what my Mam describes as 'ambidextrous'.

Mother and I live together in companionable harmony. I have my interests, she has hers. The Open University takes up some of my spare time, but within the community I seem to have become the all-purpose Secretary-type. I play tennis at the Darlington Memorial Centre Tennis and Bowls Club where I am the Secretary of the tennis section. A different group, no athletes amongst them, meet once every four weeks to discuss our 'Book of the Month' and I seem to have been left with the job of ad hoc Secretary of that organisation as well; arranging venues and sourcing the cheapest copy of the volumes we criticise. Also, because I work at the Bank, I have been brought into the Investment Club set up by the landlord of the Bull to act, again, as the Secretary. This is one of my most arduous tasks. I need to produce a list of the Club's stocks and shares every month and members become angry if my beautifully typed schedule does not show the most up-to-date prices. For goodness sake. I am a bank clerk, not a stockbroker or a sweet talking financial adviser, but I carry on as I have £1000 invested in the fund – and do not seem to be able to say 'no'.

And then there are the Players.

Having told you what I do outside of banking hours, and even inside of Morris Minors, I must repeat that despite such frantic activity, that continuous round of human contact, I am very shy: very shy indeed. Reg must have hypnotised me, but that cannot be right. He had about as much charisma as a packet of cornflakes. Perhaps he slipped something into my ginger beer shandy? Whatever, I am timid to the point of being nearly invisible. When the sun is shining, I often look behind me to see if I cast a shadow. It is not fair. I am slim, have long blonde hair and a 36 inch bust. I am 5'5" in my stocking feet with sparkling white teeth and wide blue eyes, but no worthwhile man in my life.

After telling you about me, I do not propose to take up the whole of my first chapter introducing the full cast of characters in the little saga I am about to relate. Ingrid, our tutor, tells us to keep the reader wanting more but having already given you a taste of our local and humourless Morecambe and Wise, the permanent Chairman and our indispensable Director, I have decided at this stage to add a little flesh to the bones of what has already been revealed.

Trevor Jointing needs no addition of flesh to his ample form. He is big, he is loud, he is supercilious and he is retired. Retired from the commercial world that is, but not the retiring type. He sits on the Bench, as he tells us interminably and fears for the future of the youth of our nation. I truly believe he would like everyone to enter this world fully grown, aged sixty seven and voting Conservative. He once offered himself as a local candidate, but did not even get called for an interview. For a while, after such an aberration as he called it, he talked about joining the Lib Dems. No one knows what he did in his working life. Something in the City, but I suspect that if that something had been significant, we would have heard all about it; more than once. He did one day let it slip that he had been born in Bermondsey. After retiring he bought Timberland House that must have set him back around half a million quid, so he has money. From the family, he says. I decided his father had been a porter at Covent Garden who had won the Irish Sweepstake and died before he could piss it all away in the urinals attached to his local pubs.

I did not of course acquaint Trevor with my theory or, that as a boy, I bet he was called 'Trev'. If named after his boozy father, the title of 'Trev the Bev' comes to mind.

The bonny Trev has lived amongst us for the last ten years or so. From the way he acts, and the way we feel, it could have been all of his life, and ours. His progress through the Rotary Club has been just as rapid as with the Players. During his first year he ran the bar. Not very well, if I recall, but by year two he was the Chairman. His wife is Dorothy. Dot as a girl, I'll wager. She is even more diseased with delusions of grandeur than her husband. She is always in the audience for the last night but other than that she considers amateur dramatics too plebeian for her. I decided she had been a barmaid when Trevor wooed her. Dot and Trev. Sounds like a music hall act, does it not.

Why do organisations like ours attract such people? You may have detected a hint of prejudice in my descriptions to date but I suppose he is fairly adept at chairing our meetings, no one other than he is allowed to waste time, and he does have gravitas. He would have made a splendid Alderman Helliwell in *When We Are Married*, but our Chairman always stays well this side of the footlights. Best I can say, he is harmless and does not generally interfere in the productions.

On the other hand, Ambrose is important in the scheme of things. We can manage very well without a Trev but someone who is prepared to be the Director is essential. He is short of stature, redheaded and has small feet. Perhaps that is sufficient to explain his most prominent characteristic; occasional bouts of apocalyptic rage. When he is not satisfied with what is being attempted on stage he bounces up and down on his tiny and highly polished brown brogues, moving on to a rhythmic bending of the knees and then climaxing with a series of little jumps: never less than five. At this point he closes his eyes, tightly clenches his fists, takes a deep breath and then bellows at the poor unfortunate performer who has wound him up. Precisely. He is like one of those toys with a key protruding from its back. Turn the key and the toy soldier, or whatever it is, throws up the arms in a staccato salute or walks round the nursery in a circle. If you should enter Stage Left, instead of Right, and the jumping begins, your best course of action at this point is to retrace your steps and exit Stage Left and let the volatile creature out front direct his torrent of words at a deserted stage: deserted, that is, because at the first sign of a bending of the knees the experienced members of the cast take a coffee break. Or have a fag.

In contrast, his wife is tall and thin but as serene as a mill pond. She was Head Girl when I got to St Mary's; Iris Pottinger, now Mrs Ambrose Percy. She is so self-effacing her visiting cards identify her as Mrs Ambrose Percy. If I was his wife, God forbid, I would want to keep as much of my own identity as I could.

The Pottingers have run the travel agency in the Market Square for generations. Our Ambrose landed on his feet; Iris had no brothers so he now runs the business and if you are looking for a weekend in Paris or Brighton, he will direct one of his associates to arrange it for you. However, if you are Alison Street, Ambrose will attend to the matter personally and even go with you if he can. He has a reputation as the town's Lothario but I am not sure how he earned such an accolade. He has certainly never propositioned me. Except for my diffidence, I might have tested that situation and wandered into the agency, *sans* bra, to see if I might catch his attention as I energetically turn over the travel brochures while bending low over his desk.

He is nowhere near as pompous as Trev. In fact, Ambrose is in the Society because the theatre suits his personality and he likes being the Director since then he is in charge. I am not sure what has the priority; a genuine love of the stage or the urge to be the Commander-in-Chief. Trevor is a member for prestige purposes but for our little redhead, I think he really enjoys it. Perhaps it is glib of me to call them a double act and at the same time make reference to Morecambe and Wise. Are our two funny? One is large, of Oliver Hardy proportions while the other's frame is slight, like Stan's, but are they comedians? Possibly this production of *Private Lives* will provide an answer to that question. But for now, and before we reach the action proper, I shall give you a couple of examples of the Director at work in previous productions. Firstly, *When We Are Married*. You know the one. Three couples are celebrating their silver wedding when it is discovered that the clergyman at the church where all of the ceremonies took place was not licensed and they have not therefore been legally wed at all.

In addition to Priestley's words, Ambrose attempted to spice up the action. He often tried this, not always successfully: a suggestion that Chekhov's most famous play be transferred to an apple orchard in Kent was killed at birth.

In the Priestly one, he tried to give one of the men from one of the couples, and one of the women in another, some business that was intended to suggest that they were delighted with the news that the marriages had never properly taken place and, when no one was looking, they would be in a broom cupboard together in a brace of shakes. A mistake. The male participant in this nonsense was George Thurston Brown but Helen soon put paid to that foolish piece of baloney. That was bad enough but during the early directorial process Ambrose could never remember who was supposed to be married to whom and as the cast were not too sure either, the first rehearsals nearly drowned in a sea of confusion. Perhaps he had been working too hard at the time, or Iris had finally given him some fatherly duties to perform, but none of that could excuse the unreasonable tantrum during *Spring and Port Wine*.

This is the play where the patriarch insists that his daughter eats the herring provided for her tea. When the young lady refuses, the father instructs that no other food will be provided then, or at any subsequent meal, until the fish is eaten. A man named Peter Tomlinson was playing the father. He has since left the district but not because of his clash with Ambrose. Early during rehearsals he mistakenly referred to the herring as a kipper. Ambrose exploded. Peter, he was quite a guy, I rather fancied him, thought such an outburst was unjustified so at every other rehearsal he substituted kipper for herring and continued to do so up to, and including, the Dress Rehearsal. I thought we would have to get medical help for our furious Director. Even on the second night of the run the intrepid Tomlinson said 'kerring' on more than one occasion. Of course, if Ambrose had acted like a rational human being at the time of the first error, that would have been the end of it, but as far as the backstage people were concerned we enjoyed the fun. Indeed, Joan Smith, who was doing props for the play, brought to the Dress Rehearsal both herring and kipper and swapped them around when Ambrose was not looking.

At this point, a diversion to one of my other interests, the Open University where I am studying Creative Writing. Roger Scotland is in my tutorial group but, par for the course, he ignores me. I am sure this information will have intrigued you. Not Roger Scotland's appalling manners, but the subject of my extramural studies. I have said, in reference to this idiosyncratic account of an inconsequential piece of amateur theatre, that no one will ever read it. What I mean by 'no one' is the generality of the public, particularly the burghers

of Great Selsdon, but I am contemplating letting some of my words
out of the box when dealing with the Life Writing assignment I am
required to submit for the Open University. A minor confession. I
have already submitted part of Chapter One for the comments of
Ingrid, subject to it being kept under lock and key. I do not want it to
be read out, not one sentence, at our tutorial meetings. Her response
was not very flattering, but then she is of German extraction and
so will not be familiar with the subtleties of the British amateur
stage. Or any other for that matter. She seemed unfamiliar with the
works of George Bernard Shaw, or the 'Angry Young Men', but as
dramatic literature is not included in the course, her ignorance is
perhaps immaterial.

What is included, as well as Fiction and Life Writing, the term
the OU uses for biography and autobiography, is Poetry. I wrote the
following about Ambrose but then thought I had better not send it
to Ingrid even though, after *Private Lives,* I did think of seeing if I
could persuade the Editor of the local rag to include it in its weekly
publication, preferably next to the long-running advertisement
inserted by Pottingers.

If you feel like pottering around Europe, consult Pottingers.

You think I made that up. I promise you, that is one of their taglines. Surely even Ambrose cannot be that gauche. I thought of an
improvement.

For all your travel, from Spain to Turkey.
Go to Pottingers and see Ambrose Percy.

But, back to my lyrical masterpiece.

His hair is as red as the Post Office van.
And I'm told his middle name's Peter.
He is not what you call an equable man.
In fact his temper is all of a teeter.

The shoes are polished as an elephant's tusk.
But the feet so enclosed much smaller.

When herring was kipper he came fit to bust.
Like a net full of fish on the trawler.

Oh Alison, Alison, you don't know your words.
But forgive you, forgive you, I must.
When I see you on stage I'm away with the birds,
And consumed with unquenchable lust.

I did not get very good marks from Ingrid for my Poetry submission, even though it was infinitely superior to the Ambrose ditty.

When informing you of my various part-time honorary positions, I concluded with the remark, 'And then there are the Players'. Well, to be more, accurate, the Great Selsdon Amateur Dramatic Society who are often referred to as 'the Players' and which illustrious organisation has been running for twenty five years. Last Christmas we broke with a near quarter of a century of tradition and presented *The Wizard of Oz*. For some years dear Vera Roberts has coped quite adequately with the pantomime –while Ambrose potters off to spend Christmas in Prague or tries to break both his legs at Gstaad – but some bright spark on the Committee suggested a change for a change; and so the poor lady had to find a Dorothy who could sing.

I need to come clean. Trevor was away at the nearest BUPA hospital where, according to his reports, the most famous orthopaedic surgeon in Europe was removing our Chairman's arthritically diseased right knee and replacing it with the latest substitute fashioned in trillium – or titanium – or some such name as that. Evidently its main use is to provide the outer skin for spacecraft, according to Trev.

This fascinating medical information is mostly irrelevant, except to explain why our Vice-Chairman, George Thurston Brown, was in charge and how I was able, as if by magic, to persuade all present to do away with Aladdin and Puss-in-Boots and welcome the Wizard. I will tell you about George later, but on this occasion he woke from his torpor and supported the proposal. In fact he became sufficiently lively that when I prepared the minutes of the meeting I was able to record, with a certain degree of authenticity, that George had himself proposed this extraordinary break with convention. Trevor was not best pleased about this, but even he could not arrange an about-turn when it was already fully cast and posters had been printed.

There were no difficulties with casting the three codgers Dorothy meets on the Yellow Brick Road. The one who sings *If I only had a brain*, the Scarecrow, was the easiest part to fill. Thomas Sandford did not have much of a singing voice but the absence of an organ of intelligence was unquestionable. He ran the Post Office: not one of our regulars but some years before he had something of a triumph as one of the Ugly Sisters. Type-casting I thought. All right, he is not too unhandsome nor exactly the village idiot, but I tested him out once and asked how much it was to send a letter, first class, to Mars. He looked it up in his Manual of Post Office Regulations but while doing so I beat a hasty retreat. The next time I was in his presence he gave me a rather quizzical look but then dealt with the renewal of my motor vehicle licence most efficiently. Surprisingly, I can be a trifle audacious sometimes. He made an excellent brain-less Scarecrow.

The role of the Cowardly Lion was filled by the supposedly most courageous member of the community, the local police-constable. In actual fact no one knows how brave he could be; violence is rare in our part of the world and the Saturday night crowd at the Bull are only noisy in the friendliest of ways. To complete the trio, I would like to report that Mr Stubbs, who runs the hardware shop next door to the butchers, was drafted in as the Tin Man, but not so. That honour went to Ralph Slater, who occupies the other cashier position alongside me at the Bank.

And then Vera's triumph, or nearly so, was to persuade Alison Street to be Dorothy. She looked so charming in blue ankle socks and with red ribbons in her hair that matched the famous red shoes, but it was difficult for these attractions to hide her lack of a singing voice. Or should I describe it as a vocal ability so many, many miles removed from the faintest pastiche of a Judy Garland that on the night I saw the show the lacklustre rainbow sounded extremely far away and the chimney tops were way out of sight. Nevertheless, Vera did the best she could and I think Alison charmed most everyone. She was so sweet and demure; you could almost believe she was brought up in Kansas and had a dog called Toto. Pity Ambrose missed it.

As a result of Vera's success with the Wizard I began to whisper into some ears that we should try *Oliver* for the Christmas after next: for this Yuletide, *Cinderella* is already at the starting blocks. When Trevor gallantly limped into the Chair at the next meeting of the Committee after his life-threatening operation, he expressed some pained regret that the customary practice of the Society had been thrown out of the window; and intoned that it should never happen again. I think Vera approved of his stand. She was more at ease with pussy cats than little boys singing *Food, Glorious Food* or Fagin and his crew opining that *You've Got to Pick a Pocket or Two*. Pity, I could see Ambrose as Fagin, sporting red whiskers, in his first on-stage appearance.

But let me tell you something about 'dear Vera', as everyone calls her. She is a reformed alcoholic. Her early history is a secret but I have determined she was a chorus girl who then ran a nightclub with her first husband. She might have been the inspiration for John Betjeman. Not very likely, but *Sun and Fun. Song of a Nightclub Proprietress* is one of his most evocative works: see the first and last verses.

> I walked into the nightclub in the morning;
> There was kummel on the handle of the door.
> The ashtrays were unemptied,
> The cleaning unattempted,
> And a squashed tomato sandwich on the floor.
>
> There was sun enough for lazing upon beaches,
> There was fun enough for far into the night.
> But I'm dying now and done for,
> What on earth was all the fun for?
> For I'm old and ill and terrified and tight.

Vera is in fact hale and hearty; reticent about her past but forthcoming about her drink problem. Probably that is why she is cured. She arrived at Spring Cottage with Fred, her second husband, about a dozen years ago. Both are in their early sixties and seem to be comfortably well off. He has retired from a job at the Gas Board and now tends the garden and plays bowls while Vera involves herself in good works, which in due course included directing the annual pantomime. My mother is very fond of both of them. Fred likes his pint and is often on the fringe of her riotous Saturday night bunch, with Vera in tow. She drinks a strange mixture of tonic water, soda and Angostura bitters.

Other than Roger's wife, Vera is the only other member of the Society that exhibits any evidence of a past connection with the professional stage. I have suggested as a chorus girl but it must have been more than that. One or two of our members have real talent, but at the amateur stage level. This includes Ambrose, who performs as well as he does through a genuine interest in the theatre and the force of his personality, but Vera is different. As I have said, she does not talk about her past but in view of her ability she must have been connected with the stage at a rather more senior level than as a member of the chorus, as was clear from the time of the first pantomime. Amongst anyone in the Players, she certainly knew what she was doing.

"Why don't you challenge Ambrose? You are a much better Director than he is."

"But, my love, he enjoys it so and I'm happy with the Dick Whittington's of this world. Do you not notice? The pantomimes are always less trouble than the straight plays. Look at *The Winslow Boy*, or when two of the three sisters had a quarrel and walked off the stage at the time of the Dress Rehearsal. Our pieces are supposed to be fun and so everybody relaxes and if someone forgets a few lines, the audience just laugh. If the same thing happened during the serious stuff, Ambrose would have a fit and that Roger Scotland would be rude to everyone."

"I can see that, but what about the challenge? Why not some Shakespeare?"

As I said this a deathly hush seemed to descend upon the pair of us as we sat by ourselves in the Snug at the Bull. The Great Selsdon Amateur Dramatic Society and William S. Not very likely.

"Let me tell you, in earlier days I donned some trousers and enjoyed being Bottom in a very adventurous production, but let's face it, we don't have enough people, or a big enough stage."

"I accept that, but what about a modest musical? *The Boy Friend* for instance."

"You know that is daft. How many can sing? Not the pretty Alison for sure – but she did her best in the Wizard."

I capitulated. In any case it is a much more interesting story if Ambrose is the Director. We would not want our little efforts to glide smoothly towards opening night with no upsets, as they might do if Vera was in charge.

I make light of my role in the Society but the theatre fascinates me and I am quite knowledgeable about it as well. I try to visit the London stage once or twice a year. Reg was never very interested but usually I arrange excursions with Vera as a companion and once or twice, when she could find a babysitter, Iris Percy has joined in my little outings. I suggested to Ambrose that Pottingers might add theatre trips to their catalogue of exciting holidays and events but when he showed little enthusiasm I did not persist. Even if he had been tempted I can imagine what would have been booked; the Whitehall farces and the 96th season of *Les Mis*. Let me not denigrate the Hugo musical. I have seen it twice and was moved on both occasions but enough is enough and I seem to have become more of a fan of Stephen Sondheim. When I am reincarnated as the lead singer in the Great Selsdon Music Society, my crowning glory will be as Carlotta singing, *I'm Still Here.*

Good times and a bum times,
I've seen them all and, my dear,
I'm still here.

Being a wallflower does not seem to inhibit my imagination except that in Carlotta's past she danced in her scanties, something even my most vivid dreams cannot envisage.

As a result of my passion, if that is not too strong a word, I have accumulated a substantial library of theatrical books, including play scripts. The words used during all of the productions by the Society nestle in my bedroom bookcase; at least all of those since I joined. My copy of *Private Lives* is in a Methuen volume of collected plays that includes, alongside our current production, *Bitter-Sweet, The Marquise* and *Post Mortem*. I doubt if these will ever grace our stage, and probably not many others. They do not have the appeal of *Private Lives* which, in the introduction to this volume by Sheridan Morley, is described as 'a guaranteed copper-bottomed audience-puller that had temporarily rescued countless repertory companies from the throes of a bad season'. That was written in 1998 but I think, despite our many vicissitudes, we proved his words to be just as accurate today. We had full houses nearly every night.

Needless to say, we are not the Theatre Royal, Drury Lane. Our venue is the Church Hall, if you are talking to the Rev Bob, or the Village Hall with most everyone else. The Church might own the building but it would be as ruined as Riveaux Abbey if it was not for our citizens, believers and atheists, who find the cash to keep it wind and watertight. Of course, the word 'village' is a misnomer. We are a small market town but the 'Village Hall' seems more appropriate for the modest premise where we play, for four nights only, in an auditorium that can seat a maximum of three hundred punters, desperate for a spot of culture.

There are not too many other attractions in Great Selsdon. The Music Society, using the same venue as we do, presents a Gilbert and Sullivan every year and intermittently there is some music at the Church, a trio or an organ recital. We used to have a cinema but the building is now only open at weekends and on Mondays, for bingo, but if you are so inclined, there are two minor stately homes within half an hours drive that you might visit. Coward had already made fun of such as them.

> The baby in the guest wing
> Who crouches by the grate,
> Was walled up in the west wing
> In 1428.
> If anyone spots
> The Queen of Scots
> In a hand-embroidered shroud,

We're proud
Of the Stately Homes of England.

In the town itself there are a number of pubs but most of these are now more eating houses, gastro-some thing or other, without the atmosphere of being local to the adjoining populace. Thank goodness the Bull limits its gastronomy to packets of crisps and the occasional pork pie.

In the Sheridan Morley introduction he emphasises that *Private Lives* contains little action, except for a fight at the end of Act Two and another at the end of the play, and there are really no other characters but the two couples who are faced with, in Morley's words, 'a technical exercise of incredible difficulty even for accomplished light comedians'. As my tale unfolds, we shall see if we overcome these difficulties.

Chapter Two

The Auditions

IF I was intent on giving you the most complete insight into the 'Life and Times of the Great Selsdon Amateur Dramatic Society' by describing one of their productions, I might have chosen a play with more characters. Except for the maid, who speaks no English, the cast of *Private Lives* comprises two young to middle-aged upper class couples and no one else. You would have met more of our members if I was to describe that catastrophic presentation of *When We Are Married* but I am attracted to the Coward play because it is so witty and because it concerns 'affairs of the heart', a subject close to my own romantic nature. And yet, on reflection, you may better be able to understand the process involved in an audition meeting if I first give you a taste of a play with a larger array of actors and the Priestley one is as good an example as any. Even more importantly, it will provide a preliminary introduction to a number of the most active members of the group, many of whom are involved, either on or off the stage, with my *Private Lives* story.

Perhaps I need to go further back. After the auditions for *Spring and Port Wine* Roger complained, vociferously, that during those auditions he had been cast as the father and not a relative newcomer, that upstart Peter Tomlinson. Ambrose resisted, although as matters turned out it might have been wiser to have chosen Roger, but because of the fuss the Committee decided that in the future the Secretary

28

should be present and prepare a minute of what took place. I did not see how this would avoid mix-ups like the one over Roger and Peter. That was just a case of our leading man assuming he would, as a matter of course, be given the best part but I was glad to attend these gatherings that are often just as much fun as the finished product.

All of the Committee members had been in favour of the Priestley drama; 'our sort of play' was Trev's comment.

"Amusing and down-to-earth, without bad language or innuendoes."

I was astonished that he knew one end of an innuendo from 'tother'. As you will see, I am already getting into my Yorkshire persona for this one. And what was the reference to rabbits but an innuendo. The drunken photographer tells the young maid Ruby that she is too young to understand the complexities of married life, to which she replies:

I've eard that afore, but nobody ever tells me what it is I'm too young to understand. An for years me brother kept rabbits.

The Chairman's remarks continued.

"And, it's only one set."

Someone has been briefing him, I thought. Yes, no change of set and plenty of parts for the regulars. From comments he made I was not sure Ambrose knew the play but he accepted, with grace and humility, the usual offer that he should be the Director.

"Well done, Ambrose, old chap. Another triumph, I'm sure, but don't forget to include our charming Secretary in the auditions; proper minutes must be kept so we have no arguments afterwards."

At this point he probably looked at Roger and gave him that fat-lipped smile of his but I did not observe any facial movements because I had lowered my head at the words 'charming Secretary'. Was he drunk, or had his wife been kind to him the night before?

There was a good turnout at the audition; clearly the generality of our members agreed with the positive comments made by the Committee. Even Vera was there, together with Fred. She is such a great asset to the Players. As I have already said, she has a real feeling for the stage, is not temperamental and fun to work with. At least, that is my view, but I am not sure how Ambrose felt. She told me

Fred had a match that evening at the Bowls Club – it was some final or other – and she wanted to be there for his anticipated triumph. I told Ambrose this and although there was a flash of annoyance he was relatively calm when Vera herself opened the proceedings before the Director had chance to deliver his usual speech about protocol and procedures.

"Mr Director. Thay can put me down for that Mrs Northrop, by gum. I'd be right gradely in that part – and I'se bought me sen a new pinny."

Well, that is what it sounded like to me but I do not think Ambrose understood a word of it. She then continued in her normal voice.

"Sorry my dear Ambrose, but I have to rush off with Fred. He's the Captain, so has to be early. Of course, if anyone else would like to do Mrs N, only too pleased to step aside. I expect it will be hotly contested. It's a lovely part. Goodnight and good luck. Bye-bye everyone."

It was a long meeting. By the time Ambrose got round to casting Mrs Northrop the majority who were still awake were tired and grumpy. Although Tricia indicated that she would be prepared to try for it, Ambrose had already pencilled in Vera's name on the strength, so I thought, of her performance as Muriel Wickstead in Alan Bennett's *Habeas Corpus*. I smile to myself as I recall her standing in front of an imaginary mirror, adjusting her hair, or a hat, and exclaiming that she gets to look more like the Queen Mother every day. For me that was one of the classic moments in the whole of our repertoire.

In addition to the decision to cast Vera there was not too much discussion about who would play Nancy, described as, 'an attractive girl in her early twenties'. I thought Alison would have been better cast as Ruby but Ambrose was not prepared to move Miss Street from her pedestal of perfect female pulchritude and so that was that. Two down, but a lot to go.

Naturally, the competition was keenest for the three couples and it is at this point I should tell you about our in-house Lunts. Sorry, I am going back a bit. As some of you will know the Lunts were a husband and wife acting team, Alfred Lunt and Lynn Fontanne, who enjoyed long careers, mostly on the Broadway stage. They were considered to be the greatest acting couple in American theatrical history: they retired in 1960 but on reflection, is it reasonable or relevant to compare this famous pair with the Scotlands?

Do you know the short Rattigan play, *Harlequinade*? A Donald Wolfit type and his wife are backstage rehearsing *Romeo and Juliet*. Neither is young enough to be remotely appropriate for Shakespeare's lovers, but this pair always gets the principal parts. If they were doing Arthur Miller's, *All My Sons*, this couple would rewrite it so as to have the main conflict between a father and a daughter. Well, we have a similar pair: Roger and Brenda Scotland are our precocious leading actor and his lady. On occasions some members have objected to their pivotal position in the Society but these acts of dissent have been somewhat half-hearted of late and for some time now it has become holy writ that they get the best roles.

This irritates me, and those few others, but they are the best performers in the company – and let no one gainsay the fact. We did *Harlequinade* last year, partnered with *The Browning Version*, and guess who played Crocker Harris and his wife? Amazingly I had a small part in *Harlequinade* – just two lines – but on three nights out of four Roger cut across my speech and it was lost to my friends in the audience who were eagerly awaiting my maiden performance. He is not a favourite of mine.

Ambrose is, for the most part, a pragmatist where our supreme couple are concerned. He really has little option but accept the inevitable and so the first twenty minutes after Vera's departure were taken up with a debate as to which of the husbands would be played by Roger and which of the wives by Brenda. If the choice had been mine I would have opted for the initially timorous Herbert Soppit and Annie Parker, described by Priestley as, 'a hopeful kind of woman', but perhaps the Scotlands are not as perceptive as I am. After more fruitless discussion, Roger was cast as the Alderman, superior to a mere Councillor or a plain Mr, while Brenda played Mrs Helliwell, clearly the most important lady as she was the hostess of that disastrous Silver Wedding party.

On this occasion Roger was making all of the running without his wife being involved and so, if he wanted to play the Alderman, he rather expected Brenda to fall in line and play Mrs Helliwell even though Annie Parker is the better role. He did not always get his own way, she can be as strong and forceful as he, and I thought that if she had been on the Committee she may well have supported *Who's Afraid of Virginia Woolf.* Roger failed to see that George and Martha are one of the finest married-couple portraits in modern theatre; Brenda would not have made that mistake.

To be fair to Ambrose, while dealing with the demands of the Scotlands he conducted proceedings as though all parts were open to everyone, but when our prima donnas were settled to their satisfied advantage, he was then able to begin in earnest. George Thurston Brown saw himself as the aggressive Councillor Parker, but Ambrose was less certain.

"George. You are beginning to sound a little more domineering but, to be frank, you still put me in mind of a shy pupil teacher or a new subaltern in the Mess. Try it again. More aggression. Behave like the Colonel. From the part where he wants to sack the organist."

Why should I be careful? I'll tell him to his face, what I've said behind his back. He never ought to have been appointed, and now
… …

"No, no, my dear fellow. Still not bold enough. Get really angry. Sound as though you are going to out-face your wife's lover."

At that, silence fell on the gathered flock.   Helen Thurston Brown. Did Ambrose know something we did not?

If there was a boyfriend in the wings, George was too set in his ways to go looking, but whether Ambrose's remark had an effect, or whether he decided he really wanted this part, George puffed out his cheeks, raised his voice a decibel or two and, to Ambrose's satisfaction, became Councillor Albert Parker. I think it was the moustache that persuaded. It is luxuriant and George is excessively fond of it. When he cannot think of anything to say at meetings of the Committee, which is quite often, he strokes the ginger growth on his top lip and smiles at the same time.

Except for his irritating inertia, he is essentially a nice man; a gentleman in the true sense of the word, as my story will reveal. Not very bright, but then he is an ex-soldier, a profession that in my experience does not require too much by way of brainpower, or initiative. Or perhaps that only applies to the Territorial Army. Reg was in the TA. George reached the dizzy heights of Captain but he never uses the appellation. I wonder if it was the moustache that was responsible for him capturing Helen. She is a very different kettle of fish. (Where does that expression come from? Am I obsessed with fish?)

Helen is tall and slim and has rather large feet; by no means a beauty, but she is smart. Her first husband left her, we do not know the full story, and she seemed to have taken George on the rebound, as it were; he had just retired from the forces. There are no children and, as far as I can tell, George's occupation seems to consist of reading the *Daily Express* every day, except on Sunday when he listens to the Reverend Bob, and walking through the town, going nowhere, but smoking his pipe.

Not so Helen. She inherited from her father a medium-sized printing works. I say medium-size but it is probably the single largest employer in Great Selsdon and Helen runs it with verve and efficiency. I always thought she could easily have been the Chairman of ICI. She did not think much of Trevor Jointing: saw him, like me, as the upstart he undoubtedly is, and as a result there is continuous friction within the Committee as to which firm should print our playbills and programmes. It is small change to Spire Printing, Helen's firm, but it is a matter of pride. Both she and her husband are members and Spire gives us a large discount, but Trevor was for ever suggesting we try somewhere else. I think Helen avoided joining the Committee because she thought all of them were blockheads, her husband included I suppose, but she and I are good friends. We lunch together at The George once or twice a month when we tear strips off our fellow thespians.

There is no doubt in my mind that amongst the three women, Annie Parker is the most interesting. Indeed, except for the change in behaviour by Herbert Soppit at the end of the play, she is much less stereotyped than any of the three couples and if I were an actress that would have been my choice. Helen is not as polished as Brenda Scotland but she is an intelligent woman who saw the variations in

Annie and therefore applied herself when reading for that part and was able to persuade Ambrose to choose her.

Except for the time effectively wasted with our stars, Ambrose was satisfied with progress so far to such an extent he agreed that the Rev Bob should have the small part of Fred Dyson, the newspaper reporter. He said to me, out of earshot of our cleric, there was no reason why Priestley's man of the press should not have a speech impediment. He also said it might get a few extra laughs, but I know he was not serious. Ambrose is not a cruel man.

In keeping, the Rev Bob could have been given the part of the Rev Clement Mercer, but he is not old enough. There are not many lines for this character, described as, 'a large grave clergymen' – I wondered at Priestley's adjective – and so Ambrose promoted Bill Johnson from his normal position as stagehand to the wearing of a dog collar. I was not sure how pleased Bill was about this. Not much of a churchgoer and somewhat diffident on-stage, unless he has a hammer in his hand. He is a carpenter in real life, but he accepted the role of the Rev Mercer with not too many concerns.

One of the best actors we have in the Company is Owen Ready, a foreman at Spire Printing. Pity Vera's pantomimes have not yet included *Robin Hood*; Owen would be a perfect Friar Tuck. He is a round and jolly man who gets on with everyone but in addition he has a natural ease on stage, an expressive voice and a good sense of timing. I love him. If he is not on stage he tends to run the bar at our productions. We always make the highest profit when this jovial character is mixing the gin and tonics and at this meeting no one contested his inalienable right to play Henry Ormonroyd, the tipsy photographer.

As I have said, we have more women members than men and as a result there was brisk competition for the part of Clara. Eventually Ambrose decided on George's sister Ruth, who teaches at the girl's grammar school. Where George is slow of movement, and on the uptake, his sister is a bright and pretty woman, destined to play a principal role in my account of *Private Lives*, who was liked by everyone in the Company. I admired her and was considering whether I should have my hair cut short; it suited her so well. She has a wide circle of friends and is subject to a certain amount of friendly gossip as to why she is not yet married but as I was to discover, she was determined to wait for Mr Right to come along, and to-date he has not.

The 'other woman', Lottie, was given to Owen's wife. Younger than him, contemporary of my mother's, and fond of garish clothing. As she entered the Village Hall for this audition she was wearing a yellow dress that dazzled the eye and a pair of blue suede lace-up shoes that resembled football boots. Shades of Elvis Presley. Fitted in with Lottie very well.

Alison was Nancy and she told Ambrose of a young man she knew who could play Gerald, her sweetheart in the play. Ambrose did not like the sound of this but he soon surrendered; he could deny her nothing. We still needed a young girl to play Ruby. She is supposed to be around fifteen years of age, but we had no such person at the audition. Ambrose whispered to me, would I do it? I refused, firmly but gracefully. He therefore had to end the evening with that part not cast but I later persuaded Sally Boothroyd, a junior at the Bank, to take it on. Told her it was the best route I knew for the securing of a 'young man to walk out with'. Of course I said no such thing. Bank juniors as pretty as Sally are only engaged with 'walking out' when they are leaving their current swains, but she thought the Players might be 'a bit of a laugh' – which in this production proved to be only too true.

Subject to Ambrose approving of Alison's candidate for Gerald, the cast was now complete except for Herbert Soppitt. It is an interesting role; a fairly classic example of the worm who turns. At this point I whispered into Ambrose's ear something I had heard from my mother.

Do butcher's shops generate more gossip than others? Is it the white clinical interior? Ruth had evidently formed a warm regard for one Jeremy Coxon, a widower who had recently settled in the area. His wife had been killed in a motor accident in Nigeria where he was working as an accountant with Shell and service in that 'white man's grave' had allowed him to retire when still in his very early fifties.

Too old, I thought, to be her 'Mr Right'. He joined us when he first arrived in the neighbourhood, having done some acting when overseas, and competed for the part of the father in *Spring and Port Wine*. I, for one, was glad when he was not chosen. Too sure of himself for my taste, but he had sent apologies to Ambrose for this evening; a bridge four he could not escape, so he said. I suggested to Ambrose that it might be interesting to pair him up with Ruth and our skilful Director immediately saw the challenge. Ruth would have to put aside her gentle demeanour to portray the sharp-tongued Clara and Coxon would need to tone down, at least until the last Act, his arrogant manner in portraying the henpecked Herbert. Ambrose closed the meeting, intending to phone his potential Mr Soppitt the next day. The invitation was accepted and so we were complete.

The play was cast; a satisfactory outcome but, as it happened, that was the last time the word 'satisfactory' could be used. From then on it went from bad to worse. One of the minor mishaps that occurred on opening night was when, for about two pages of text, Councillor Parker got the ladies mixed up: he took his sister to be his stage wife instead of Helen, his spouse in real life and Alice Parker on stage. Sounds confusing even as I write it down. By that time most of the audience were totally confused but Ambrose was choking with rage as the Councillor's remarks, meant for his wife, were directed at Clara Soppitt.

On the second night George missed an entrance so the three couples had to begin the vital scene where they begin to face the dilemma they are in with one of the husbands missing. Ambrose screeching out, "Where the bloody hell is George?" could be heard as far back as Row E.

There was a further disaster with the Reverend Bob, cast as the brash young reporter, Fred Dyson. It was Ambrose's fault; he should never have included our vicar in the first place. Willing as he was his stutter began to manifest itself as soon as the make-up lady started to apply the foundation coat to his pale face and by the time he made his entrance on stage, he was incoherent. His first line was particularly unfortunate.

Evening, Miss Holmes. How d'you do? This is Mr Henry Ormondroyd, our photographer.

Owen, playing Ormondroyd, cut Bob off in the middle otherwise there would have been no progress, but Alison as Nancy did not have the same experience and she stood and waited patiently for Dyson to finish before she spoke. At one point I thought Ambrose was about to order the curtain to be lowered, but the splendid Owen pressed on and, in effect, projected all of the lines, or the sense of them, of Dyson, Nancy and Gerald – her young man – before there was the welcome exit of both the tongue-tied reporter and the brilliant photographer with the latter's line:

They're keeping a very nice drop of beer down at the Lion now.

By this time it was our Director who needed a drink, preferably a very large whisky, but he would probably have been unable to indulge because, in the wings, he was shaking with silent rage. I was concerned at this point that he was about to punch the clergyman on the nose but as he moved forward I was able to restrict his passage by the raising of my shapely right leg. I was the prompt for that production.

At the end of Act Two, just when it is revealed that it is Helliwell who had promised to marry Lottie, there are some further visitors.

RUBY [importantly]: Mayor o' Cleckleywyke, Yorkshire Argus,
Telegraph, and Mercury.
[MAYOR enters, carrying case of fish slices, with REPORTERS
behind.].
MAYOR [pompously]: Alderman and Mrs Helliwell, the Council and
Corporation of Cleckleywyke offers you their heartiest congratulations on
your Silver Wedding and with them this case of silver fish slices.
[He is now offering the case to MARIA, who has suddenly sunk down
on the settee and is now weeping. She waves the case away, and the
bewildered MAYOR now offers it to HELLIWELL, who has been
looking in exasperation between his wife, LOTTIE and the MAYOR.
HELLIWELL takes the case and opens it without thinking, then seeing
what is in it, in his exasperation, shouts furiously.]
HELLIWELL: An I told yer before Fred – I don't like fish.
[Quick curtain.]

Ambrose had been hard-pressed to find someone to play the Mayor and in desperation had turned to Simon Duncan, one of our regular set-builders. Not very bright, a cleaner at Spire Printing, but willing. Dressed in an old frockcoat Doreen had found amongst our costumes he looked the part, and, to be fair to him, he had learnt the few lines he had to deliver. Problem was on the opening night he mixed up the couples and tried to present the fish slices to Annie Parker. Helen attempted to indicate that he should be addressing Brenda but he failed to recognize this and dumped the case into the arms of George. Without thinking, George opened the case which left Roger with a dilemma: how does he deliver the last line and get the curtain down? He did well and came out with, 'But you don't like fish, Albert.'

The next night Simon delivered the present to the correct parties but as Maria waved the case away, the poor unfortunate chap dropped the box and a clatter of cutlery echoed around the silent actors on stage. This time Roger reacted by kicking one or two of the fish slices across the stage that added some emphasis to the curtain line about not liking fish. At the time of the first incident, Ambrose was in the Director's box at the back of the auditorium; he had retired there after failing to attack the nose of the Rev Bob during Act One, and as the curtain fell on Act Two, those seated at the rear of the Hall would have heard the sound as he beat his head against the glass panel dividing him from the paying public.

In addition to prompt, I was drafted in to help Eustace Simpson who was in charge of publicity. He is the Editor of *The Record*, our local weekly that we are all so proud of. It boasts having been published continuously for one hundred and fifty years. Eustace explained to me that he had just employed a new reporter who had been allocated responsibility for the arts and special events, such as car boot sales and WI coffee mornings. Evidently this young man was anxious to write an extended and incisive review on *When We Are Married* that would be so interesting it would be featured on the front page.

"Not very likely, May, but he is keen so I'm giving him his head. No experience, but has a nice manner."

"Bully for you, Mr Editor."

"And so, I've told him to interview you for background material on the Players. You seem to know what's going on around here, but be gentle won't you. No scandals please. *No Sex Please, We're British.*"

Eustace must have thought that was being very witty. I did not; neither did I care for the fact that once again I am lumbered with jobs like this. I could just imagine the guy. Delusions of being an intellectual and 'arty' as well. Long hair and a spotty face but I was pleasantly surprised to find that Adrian Spencer was nothing of the sort and I enjoyed our little chat, even though I did rather lecture him.

He was younger than me but that could not explain why I became so outgoing with a total stranger. It had never happened before. First of all I told him that if he was going to write about the play he must be sure and actually witness a performance. At this he looked at me as though I was losing my wits. I continued and told him the apocryphal story of a reporter who filed his review without bothering to go to the theatre, a building that burns down during opening night. I went on and compared this unfortunate occurrence to the epic blunder by the *Chicago Tribune* who printed, 'Dewey defeats Truman' when such was not the case. The young reporter appeared to be unacquainted with either of these stories and continued to look at me as though he thought I was slowly moving into an incipient stage of lunacy.

I asked him if he had read anything by Priestley. At school he must have studied science rather than the humanities because he began to talk about the man who is credited with the discovery of oxygen. More recent than that, I said. JB: broadcaster, pipe smoker, writer of plays and professional Yorkshireman. At that point he grinned. Was he pulling my leg? For some reason he then told me, at some length, about his younger sister who when at school had been Peaseblossom in *A Midsummer Night's Dream* and how their mother had made the wings. The amount of background material he accumulated at that meeting must have been miniscule, but he seemed satisfied.

But that is enough about *When We Are Married.* My appointed task is to now take you on the four months journey that *Private Lives* enjoyed from the decision to turn to 'the ever dependable Coward' until that unusual last night party but, as I intended, this Priestly diversion has allowed me to introduce a wider range of our members, even if only sketchily. Let me therefore, at this point in my chronicle, tell you a little more about the Scotlands.

I was prepared to accept Brenda as a leading lady, but her husband was awful. She had some dramatic training; not exactly RADA but I believe she joined the Bristol Rep as a young girl – Assistant Stage Manager initially – and then progressing towards some minor speaking parts. She therefore knew how it was done on the professional stage and I must admit that on a number of occasions the advice she has quietly tendered to Ambrose has been very useful. At the time of *Private Lives* she was, I suppose, around forty and had recovered her elegant figure after the birth of a boy and twin girls. Medium-height, auburn hair and most beautiful hands, a feature she exploited to the full during her performances. She was very aware of her talent and good looks but, to be fair, she was less conceited than she might have been. Her movements were graceful and she wore clothes well. She was rarely seen with her hair out of place or with a face devoid of makeup.

Because I so disliked her husband, I was suspicious of her: if she was as nice as I always found her to be, how did she come to link up with that fiend? Provided there was not a queue of customers, she would always chat with me about the Players whenever she came into the Bank to cash a cheque. Her voice was low, but she had the gift of articulation that carried effortlessly to the back of the Village Hall. The accent was a neutral one; her forebears were Gloucestershire farmers, but there was no hint of a West Country inflection. She never talked about when and how she had met Roger, and certainly no such information was forthcoming from him.

She was a full-time mother while Roger commuted, virtually every day, into Birmingham where he was a partner in a medium-sized firm of solicitors. They lived in one of the new houses converted from barns at Holmfield Farm and where, now and again, they entertained the local worthies. I had been included amongst the invitees at two Christmas drinks parties but what I was most keen to attend was a wedding anniversary event. That did not happen, but this omission did not deter me from determining that James, their son, had been conceived out of wedlock and that was the reason she had married such a man. We do know he had trained in Bristol so I could see him as a 'stage-door Johnny' who had seduced this attractive member of the Bristol Repertory Company, and she was caught. All fantasy no doubt as they seemed very happy together and she never muttered anything about 'promising career brought to a premature end because of an unwanted pregnancy'. This is my whimsical nature at its worst, but the probable and mundane truth that they simply fell in love did not help me towards any fondness for him, nor did my attitude change after that slip of the tongue by Jackson Tollemache.

Our Treasurer is too idle to indulge himself with indiscretions. It was not a question of principles, or morals; he was neither high-minded nor low-minded about anything and I was therefore considerably surprised at what emerged when I was trying to elicit some information from him so as to be able to prepare the Treasurer's statement that he would present at the next Annual General Meeting. Beforehand I should tell you that as far as I could tell his only enthusiasm was trying to get himself into my bed, but he did not pursue this very diligently, and he was not difficult to rebuff. Or is it just my vivid imagination once again? He was twenty years older than me with about as much personality as a cold rice pudding – without the nutmeg. I have never met his wife. In my mind I always refer to him as 'Jack-off'.

"Jackson. You said you had paid Spire for the last programme. Did they send you a receipt?"

"Sure they did. I'll look it out for you. How are we doing? In profit?"

"Seems so, but may I suggest that in your speech to the members you should reiterate how important it is to sell advertising in the programme. Valuable revenue. We missed Singletons Estate Agents last time. You know them don't you?"

"Yes, but I hear they've got themselves into a spot of bother with the Council over planning permissions at Holmfield Farm."

"Where the Scotlands live?"

"Yes."

"Is Roger involved?"

"Believe his firm acted for the developer."

"Roger. A shady deal?"

"Shouldn't think so, but how would I know? But I'll leave it to you to pop in and see old Singleton. Sure they'll be game for the next play – whats-it Lives."

Many thanks, I thought. Another lecherous old man. I could do without him trying to look down the front of my dress, but what was this about Roger, our upright and no doubt cautious man of the law? I began to open up this can of worms; if indeed there was such a receptacle with any trace of Roger therein.

As you can see from the tale so far I enjoy the written word and hence my Open University activities but, I ask myself, why had Roger Scotland signed up for the same course? When I found him at the first tutorial meeting I was, to say the least, astounded but said nothing. Neither did he. I later asked Brenda about it when perhaps a little worm did make an appearance.

"Did he tell you, Roger and I are doing the same Open University course? Creative Writing. I was surprised to see him there."

"Thinks he's going to write the 'Great British Novel' when he retires."

"Who, Roger?"

"Yes, the same."

"Perhaps he'll write about the Players. Lots of raw material there – only problem is deciding whether it should be a farce or a tragedy. Or will it be about lawyers?"

"Who knows? I rather doubt it. He's a bit fed up with the law at the moment."

"There are some wonderful lawyers in Dickins. He didn't like them much. Roger reminds me of Mr Tulkinhorn. Is he retiring soon?"

"Let's hope not. I don't want him under my feet all day, but even if he does give up the partnership, I think he would like to get into property development."

"Does he know anything about that?"

"Well, as I understand it, you don't need a lot of skill as long as you have access to a bit of capital, and know the right people."

Or, I said to myself, the 'wrong' people. So, an ambition as a novelist. I could not see that; not enough humanity in the man. No curiosity about the lesser folk but that explained why he was on my Creative Writing course and, in addition, why he might be engaged in some creative shenanigans with the planners. For the time being I stored away this little snippet of information.

We did not have as much interest from members seeking a part in *Private Lives* as with *When We Are Married* but even so, Coward is popular and the audition meeting drew a respectable crowd. I did not know then what slight Ambrose had recently suffered at the hand of Roger Scotland but our giants of the theatre were called upon to sing for their supper and show that they deserved the roles of Elyot and Amanda. I saw the exercise as a bit a sham; this play above all suited this couple more than any other I could think of outside of *Macbeth* – and the Albee one. With them heading the cast, our production of *Private Lives* was surely destined for success but Ambrose did his best to get them to prove this, particularly Roger.

He tried George Thurston Brown and Jeremy Coxon before he asked Roger to read. The bastard had already learnt most of the words.

She divorced me for cruelty, and flagrant infidelity. I spent a whole weekend with a lady called Vera Williams. She had the nastiest-looking hairbrush I have ever seen.

What wonderful lines.

"Roger, old fellow, please use the book. I do want to hear what Noël wrote and not what you think he did."

The would-be Elyot tentatively opened the script and continued, but not reading from the text which he held away from his face at the fullest stretch of his arm, like a painter calculating dimensions. An unflattering caricature of Ambrose, perhaps.

If you feel you'd like me to smoke a pipe, I'll try and master it.

Ambrose snorted.

"I beg your pardon. Those are amongst the best lines in the play. I'm sure I'm accurate."

"Be that as it may, I suggest you forget about the fact that Noël created the part for himself. We don't want a faint imitation of the Master. Be yourself, but equally languid of manner."

Roger continued.

"No, my dear fellow, a more clipped accent I think. Try and accentuate the last word of each sentence."

"Why?"

"Because then it will make you sound more like an upper class dilettante. Traces of Birmingham must not intrude."

Even when dealing with Roger Scotland I thought this was unfair, but he ignored the jibe and pressed on. Eventually Ambrose had no alternative and our Elyot was chosen but I think it was at this stage, and because he was compelled to take Roger, he had decided to consider some alternative staging for the play, but more on that later.

Casting Amanda Prynne came next. I was later to discover, courtesy of Brenda herself, that relations between she and Ambrose had rather deteriorated of late. The reason, so she alleged, was a simple one. Our gutsy Director had for years assumed that one of the perquisites of his position was that he be allowed to flirt with whichever of the female members of the cast he wished. It was harmless. Iris thought it was a big joke and most of the ladies subjected to his attention felt the same. Some might even have been flattered, but Brenda Scotland had, in recent times, begun to treat Ambrose's smiles, leers and attempted roving hands as a subject for ridicule. He was not used to such treatment and, as a result, relations between the two of them were decidedly cool.

All somewhat specious I thought, and later events revealed that there were more serious reasons for the rift between the Percys and the Scotlands. Sounds a bit like the War of the Roses, don't you think. Was the Village Hall to become the site of a modern-day Battle of Bosworth Field?

Whatever, Ambrose seemed determined that Brenda should not be allowed the part of Amanda. It was difficult. She read very well. As you know, I preferred her as an individual to her husband but I thought it was no bad thing if our glorious twosome was split up for a change. There was another motive at work. It was time to see if the pretty Alison could rise to the occasion and take on a major role but if Brenda was to be Amanda she would be too strong for Alison's Sibyl which, taken to its logical conclusion, let Miss Street in and Mrs Scotland out. In my view Alison was a mistake; an interesting gamble but I felt rather ashamed at the ditching of Brenda, particularly when she volunteered to act as the Stage Manager.

This was unheard of. Whenever there had been no suitable parts for the Scotlands in the past they bought two tickets for the show but had no further involvement with the Players until the next production came round; and if that happened to be the Christmas pantomime, their absence was an extended one. There was never any question that if they were not lighting up the stage with their vibrant presence, Brenda would be in charge of props and her haughty husband helping to build the set.

When at the end of the evening Ambrose announced that Ruth Thurston Brown would be Amanda and the part of Victor was awarded to Jeremy Coxon, Roger Scotland glowered. He was good at it, but Brenda responded, with some grace I thought.

"Ambrose, I think I could kiss you."

The object her affections, genuine or not, reddened a little – if such a change of colouring was discernible at this stage in the evening.

"The time has probably come when Roger and I should be split up. I am disappointed not to be playing Amanda. I saw Maggie Smith do it some years ago. It is a wonderful part, but I know Ruth will rise to it splendidly. As some of you know, I began at Bristol as an Assistant Stage Manager. I am a bit longer in the tooth now, Ambrose, but if you do not have a Stage Manager in prospect, I would be pleased to do it for you. And keep an eye on everyone."

At this she smiled at her husband who was still muttering under his breath. Ambrose was so surprised by this offer he could not, for a moment, find any word of response but this lapse was soon mended.

"How wonderful. What a team we shall make. This is going to be a memorable production."

And it was.

This episode confirmed my opinion of Brenda: despite her choice of husband she did have the good of the Players at heart. When they had not been involved in the past, for instance when she had not wanted to be Lady Bracknell and Roger declined either of the two young men, she had followed him into the wilderness for the duration of that production but now, as her husband was included, she stayed on board without hesitation. I had no doubt she will be a splendid Stage Manager and look forward to working with her in whatever lowly capacity I find myself.

Tricia agreed to be the maid but before the company departed, Ambrose made a speech. This was timed for the last event of the evening, rather than the first; the wily creature must have thought to cast the play before making his suggestions about staging.

"Thank you all for your support. This is one of my favourite plays and the numbers here tonight are testimony to the probability that it is equally favoured by many of you. But therein, I suggest, lies a fault. We all know it too well. Our audience will know it just as well and so, if *The Merchant of Venice* can be set on a trading floor at a twentieth century bank in the City, or members of the rival families in *Romeo and Juliet* shown as riders of motor cycles, I am proposing that our *Private Lives* should be set in Norfolk. And please do not tell me that county is very flat."

He tittered at his little joke. Everyone else in the room was struck dumb – as if we had just taken a vow of silence.

"I thought we would open at a Boarding House in Great Yarmouth. Pity we cannot introduce another character; a typical Landlady of such an establishment. Stained pinafore and hair in a snood, but we must not take too many liberties. I haven't quite worked out how the two terraces will be shown but I suppose we can envisage an up-market property that has two adjoining balconies, although this might require Elyot becoming a bit of a trapeze artist when he and Amanda come together. Never mind. Innovation. Mustn't stand still. This is the twenty-first century. Now, for the final scenes. I thought a semi-detached in King's Lynn, but with such ground-breaking changes we also need to look at the characters. We can discuss this of course, but I have in mind Elyot as a fishing trawler captain and Amanda an air-hostess – they first meet on a flight from London to Newcastle. Sibyl's career as a lap dancer has been short and sweet and Victor is the local bookie."

The silence was about to be broken, but Ambrose held up his hand.

"Of course, that's going a bit too far. We cannot give these couples any professions, current or previous. They need to be fully committed to a career in the art of falling in and out of love, but the time will be the present and Tricia will need some coaching in the accent of the Fens."

Roger's stage whisper was audible to everyone.

"Great Yarmouth. Where the bloody hell is that?"

Chapter Three

The Read-through

IT WAS Ambrose's habit to arrange a meeting of his chosen cast as soon as possible after auditions. Indeed, such a meeting was often fixed at the end of the casting procedure but with the bombshell about deserting France, Ambrose did not attempt to do so on this occasion. Normally he would have been the last to leave – he needed to have time and an arena for his harmless dalliance with the ladies – but on this occasion he slipped away as though he did not want to discuss the geography of Norfolk until his shock announcement had set in. After he had left I had the temerity to tell Roger that Great Yarmouth was famous for its bloaters and that its football team is known as 'The Bloaters'. He evinced no interest whatsoever in this intriguing piece of information and so we all scattered, with the result that I had the task of telephoning the cast members about a meeting before the end of August for the important preliminary read-through.

Although this followed hard on the heels of the auditions, there was already a change of cast. Tricia's boyfriend had told her that she was to reject being the maid again and, "If that red-headed creep will not give you a proper part, you drop out." I believe their relationship was at a delicate stage: I cannot recall whether he was trying to ditch her, or it was the other way around, but she did as he said, with or without the East Anglian accent. She would not tell Ambrose direct of course. I was the messenger; little setbacks like this so early in the process tend to bring out the worst in him. I popped into Pottingers during the lunch break to give him the news whereupon, in his agitation, he knocked over a sign advertising cheap trips to China. You can guess what happened next. As I helped him restore the sign to its upright position, I told him I would do Louise if he wanted. He looked at me rather dubiously but I could see his mind registering the fact that the principal actors would probably cut out the few lines the maid had and he therefore graciously gifted me the part. As a result, as a member of the cast I could envisage an inside berth during the stormy voyage of this eventful production.

At this first meeting – the read-through – it soon became obvious that Ambrose was going to have to call upon all of his experience to convert Alison Street into a passable Sibyl. She, Alison that is, had managed to get herself into the Nottingham Trent University from whence she emerged, two years ago, with a Third Class degree in some subject to do with Communications. This had not led to any gainful employment – she seemed to be out of communication with the commercial world – but she was able to type, after a fashion, and that enabled her to find some part-time work. She did not look for this with any liveliness. She lived with her parents, when she had not taken up temporary abode with the current object of her affections, and I suppose was typical of the young at the time; she enjoyed herself and ignored the future.

Do not get the wrong impression. Perhaps I am jealous. She is personable, polite and rather dull; unambitious and most uninterested in world affairs – but very pretty. She did not have a car and was too lazy to use a bicycle and so we all saw something of her current male companion, Tony Everington, whom she called 'Tone'. He ferried her to and from rehearsals. He was also without a car but appeared to have the means to acquire a huge Harley Davidson motorbike. She looked at her best when perched on the pillion travelling at sixty miles per hour or more with her long blonde hair streaming behind her. Sometimes this was eclipsed by a scarf that Isadora Duncan would have been proud of.

She could do no wrong in Ambrose's eyes, but by the time the curtain went up on the first night, his inconsistent tolerance had been stretched like a fully extended rubber band. It was fascinating to see it get tighter and tighter until an explosion seemed inevitable but, as I shall record, she was by no means the epicentre of the troubles.

"Now, I presume you have all taken a glance at the text, well at least your own parts. I do not address these remarks to you Roger. You probably have your lines to heart already, but for the less experienced, I must at this stage emphasise that words are king. No moves, only the lines. Alison."

"Yes Ambrose, or do I have to call you Herr Director?"

She was not without spirit on occasions.

"Ambrose will do very well my dear."

"I'm Sibyl, aren't I?"

"Yes. If you do not know which of Mr Coward's delightful characters you are to depict, learning lines becomes somewhat problematical."

"So it is Sibyl?"

"Yes, darling."

"How old is she?"

I whispered in the ear of the charming lady that she was around fifty, but Ambrose patiently told his protégé to look at the stage instructions at the beginning of the play.

"Alison. This is a read-through. Please sit down and read. You are on at the opening of the play."

Alison muttered, then looked at the book, obviously for the first time.

"Is it a big part?"

"Yes. One of the main ones."

Roger leans over towards her.

"You and I, young lady, are married. We are on our honeymoon. Are you ready for that?"

Alison looked astonished at this information. Ambrose tried to move things on.

"Thank you, Roger."

"Do I have to kiss him, or anything?"

"Alison. What did I say. Words, words, words. Just read the lines Mr Coward wrote."

There was of course no need for Louise to be present at these early meetings but Ambrose tolerated my presence and allowed me to make the tea when he gave the players a break. Nevertheless, my principal role was as an observer and even at the initial read-through I could see a number of scenarios developing.

Firstly, was Alison going to ruin the production? Secondly, why was Roger Scotland so bad tempered; surely not just because Brenda was not there? Until he became the character he was to play his manner was invariably surly or off-hand. This evening was no exception. He had the plum part in the play, for which his talents were exactly suited, but tonight he was even more unlikable than usual. I did not think he looked too well, but perhaps the jaundice was more in my eye than upon his face. With the other two, Ruth was a good choice but I could also see her as another problem. She and Jeremy Coxon had been the only people to emerge unscathed from *When We Are Married*; they had clearly enjoyed each others company during the Priestley play but that did not appear to be the case today. Something had happened. Ambrose was oblivious to these early signs of possible discord, but I thought we were all in for a bumpy ride. He then set them off on that ride.

It's heavenly. Look at the lights of that yacht reflected in the water. Oh dear, I'm so happy.

"Alison. Just a moment. I don't want to stop you right at the beginning, this is only a first read-through, but do try to mean what you say. 'Oh dear, I'm so happy.' The 'Oh dear' is affectionate. Not a sign of regret. See what I mean."

At this point the swing doors at the rear of the hall were pushed open, vigorously and noisily. Tone had arrived to ferry Alison away. Ambrose ignored the interruption and the foursome managed to reach the end of Act One without too many sighs from the Director. Roger, with an imaginary vision of Great Yarmouth in his voice, emphasised references to St. Moritz, Paris, the Casino, Toulon and earthquakes in France. Ambrose took no notice. He had his hands full with Alison.

It did get a little better. When Alison had to tell Elyot that her mother was right and that he had shifty eyes, she became moderately alive as though she really thought Roger had the same sort of eyes, as I think he does. She even chuckled at one of the early exchanges with him.

SIBYL:I don't believe you like Mother.
ELYOT:Like her! I can't bear her.
SIBYL:Elyot! She's a darling, underneath.
ELYOT:I never got underneath.

Two pages later.

ELYOT:Do you want to dine downstairs here, or at the Casino?
SIBYL:I love you, I love you, I love you.
ELYOT:Good, let's go in and dress.
SIBYL:Kiss me first.

"I thought you said I did not have to kiss him?"

"My dear Alison. It is only a little one. This is not a sex drama you know."

Want to bet, whispered Roger.

"I don't mind. But Tone might object. And he is a bit old."

"Darling, this is not real life. It's only a play. That's what we are into. Make-believe. Please let's get on."

She got quite confused at the end of the Act; clearly did not understand who Victor was and appeared to have an extraordinary ability to block out all of the lines that were not marked against the name of Sibyl which meant there was not much by way of interaction with the other players. If this persisted it was going to create a problem that might only be solved if Millicent was shipped in. Ambrose was already looking slightly apprehensive and, even more worrying, his complexion was becoming pale and cold rather than hot and crimson.

He persisted, but she made a complete mess of the lines that touched on why Elyot and Amanda had parted.

"Alison. Again. I know this is only our first meeting but this section is very important. You say you love Elyot more than Amanda loved him and you must sound as though you believe that with all your heart. You have to give Elyot the right platform for the crucial line, 'We lost each other'."

SIBYL:*I love you far more than Amanda loved you. I'd never make you miserable like she did.*

ELYOT:*We made each other miserable.*

SIBYL:*It was all her fault, you know it was.*

ELYOT *[with vehemence]: Yes, it was. Entirely her fault.*

SIBYL:*She was a fool to lose you.*

ELYOT:*We lost each other.*

SIBYL:*She lost you, with her violent tempers and carrying on.*

Alison tried again, but it was clear she was not giving Roger the opportunity to stress, 'We made each other miserable.'

"It is crucial, even at this early stage of the play, that the audience can believe that Elyot still loves Amanda so that when they run away together, from the two honeymoons, it has a semblance of possibility about it. Some credence. If this is not clear, the audience will never accept the precipitate departure at the end of the Act, and you Alison are paramount in creating this. Do you understand?"

She nodded, but no one was very confident of her answer.

Roger of course appreciated the point only too well and his grasp of the part only underlined Alison's shortcomings. Shifty eyes or not, Roger was born to play Elyot–and he knew it. Even though this was only the read-through he was already more-or-less in costume. His neatly pressed grey trousers were of a light shade, you could almost imagine them to be a pair of white ducks, and the light blue shirt was open at the neck to display a paisley-patterned cravat. Cravats were fashionable thirty years ago and he knew they are not usually worn today but Elyot would doubtless have travelled wearing one, as well as a blazer identical to that sported by Roger. It was dark, with gold buttons. There was no crest. Elyot would not have been a member of a sporting club, or any other club for that matter that had a blazer badge, unless perhaps the Garrick.

He had also done something to his hair – and his air. The former was slicked back. Can you still buy Brylcreem, I wondered? As to manner, as soon as he began to speak the lines it was clear he had left the stiff company lawyer in his office and brought to this dingy Village Hall a creature as loose as a piece of knitting that had slipped from the needles. His normal upright stance had gone and he lounged on one of the stackable chairs, the only seats available, as though it was a velvet chaise longue or a beach deckchair; a striped one. He was wearing brown suede shoes and a brightly coloured handkerchief cascaded from the top pocket of that immaculate blazer. He was Elyot.

He only pretends to kiss Sibyl – three times because she is superstitious – but follows this with the line: You really are very sweet in a perfect Elyot tone and looking at Alison as though he meant it.

When only Amanda and Victor are on stage he became Roger again; sat up straight in his chair and glared at Alison and me, alternately. He was clearly not listening to Ruth and Jeremy, or Ambrose, as he steered that pair through their first lines.

I was not sure Ruth was going to be strong enough for Amanda but by the end of Act Two and the violent parting she was beginning to prove to be a worthy opponent for Elyot. There were of course no movements attempted during this first meeting but when she came to the last line of the Act she seemed compelled to stand-up and take a pace towards Roger. Her words reverberated around that virtually empty hall.

Beast; brute; swine; cad; beast; beast; brute; devil –

This cheered Ambrose up; he very nearly applauded. I was similarly impressed. Perhaps after all she was going to be able to replace Brenda and compete for the centre of the stage with Roger?

By this time Tone was pacing up and down at the rear of the hall kicking chairs. He lined them up, one at a time, and aimed his right boot at the inoffensive article of furniture as if he was taking a penalty at Wembley. This was very irritating. Only Alison seemed oblivious but this diversion was as nothing to the intervention of Jeremy Coxon as we reached the end of the Act. What brought this about were the lines where Amanda has to give Elyot information about the address of the flat in Paris they are about to flee to.

It's in the Avenue Montaigne. I let it to Freda Lawson, but she's in Biarritz, so it's empty.

"Ambrose. I must insist we stop there. I know I'm a new member but are you really going to get Amanda to give the address of her flat as 13 Railway Cottages, Kings Lynn – or something like that – followed by the fact that she has let it to Freda Lawson but she's in Skegness, so it's empty. I applaud your attempts to modernise this thing but in *Private Lives* it's not on. You must know that. It's a slight piece that only works because these people are rich lay-abouts who do nothing except enjoy themselves, but in Great Yarmouth. I'm sorry. I think you have it wrong. Set in Norfolk, I cannot do Victor."

Ambrose was really put out. Not because of what was said, but because of who said it.

In a flash I could see the fiendish plan. He never intended to move to East Anglia. I thought something was fishy from the start. There I go, fish again. Ambrose loved the play because of the sophistication, a commodity rarely found in Great Yarmouth. How he would have loved to live the life of an Elyot; you could say he was a bit of a dilettante anyway. No, the plot required the rebellion to come from Roger. He had been able to ditch Brenda, for rather pathetic reasons already explained, and he had not wanted to cast her husband but could not avoid doing so. The clever old thing was looking for a voluntary withdrawal by our star performer and when there was a new Elyot on board, he would have dispatched Great Yarmouth into the North Sea and withdrawn in triumph to Deauville. What a scheme, but it had now backfired.

Ambrose was not a stupid man; he knew when he was beaten.

"Jeremy, old chap. Of course you're right. It was just a whim. A fancy. It has to be France. It has to be Paris. I wish to see Alison and Ruth in Dior dresses, not garments purchased from Marks & Spencer."

At this he beamed at everyone, even including me.

"Shall we get on with Act Two?"

It would appear that Tone had heard the last words and so began to whistle loudly and use his motorcycle helmet as a percussion instrument that he banged rhythmically on the exit door. At this, our Director gave Alison permission to don her leather jacket and depart.

We managed to reach the end of Act Two that night after Alison had left. I could have left with her except I wanted to see and hear the famous two hander between Elyot and Amanda that ends in their bout of fisticuffs, and so Jeremy and I stayed on. It is a wonderful play.

I thought Jeremy might have walked Ruth and me through the darkening streets of Great Selsdon but he and Roger strode off together leaving us to look after Ambrose. We got him safely to his door, where he kissed his Amanda on both cheeks and then, like one of Pavlov's dogs, did the same to me.

As we left Ambrose I could see that Ruth was temporarily agitated by the kisses she had just received. I could not understand this and I must have looked at her in a quizzical way. This prompted a surprising reaction.

"He is an old fool, but I like him. Surprised me with that wet kiss, and it made me think of the last time I was given a friendly kiss and not an ugly one."

"Sorry, how do you mean?"

"May, can we go and have a drink somewhere. The Bull is still open. We're early tonight."

"Of course."

We both drank white wine. Being the Bull I suspect it was a Chardonnay from Peru or Bulgaria but she told me she was glad to have someone like me to talk to. Her brother was hopeless, she said, and she is a bit in awe of Helen. I could understand that although I have always thought that her sister-in-law's severe demeanour was just a counter to her husband's sorry showing.

"We don't know each other very well May, but you are a caring person, I can see that, and perceptive. You don't miss much do you?"

"I do like to know what's going on but I need to make lots of assumptions because I'm too shy for a direct enquiry."

"Yes. Shy and kind. In many ways we have similar temperaments but as a teacher I have to be more assertive than perhaps my nature likes."

"Is it going well at school? Any problems there?"

"No. Despite what I have just said, I love it. My problem is very much extra-curricular."

"Jeremy?"

"Is it that obvious?"

"Perhaps only to me?"

"When we first met I was immediately attracted and, as you probably recall, it was me that suggested him for a role in *When We Are Married*. It was a good move on my part. I enjoyed acting with him and our friendship grew but then I discovered another side to him. He has spent a lot of time overseas, mostly in Africa. I suspect his wife was a rather quiet woman who allowed herself to be dominated. She was the daughter of a missionary in Northern Nigeria, but anyway, as a result he seems to have acquired some of the male superiority that is, so I read, to be found amongst African men. In short, after the Priestley play was over he invited me for dinner at his house where it soon became plain that he fully expected me to join him in his bedroom as soon as the coffee was over. I made it clear that I had no such intention and I'm afraid he became somewhat violent. Shook me and pushed me into an easy chair. I was furious. He saw it and immediately fell to his knees and apologised profusely. As he walked me back home he continued to excuse himself saying he'd been too long in the tropics and not used to the company of genteel ladies, but I was disturbed, as you can imagine."

I nodded my head.

"It was not the aggression that concerned me the most, it was the fact that he could have read the situation so wrongly. I am not attached to another man, he is also free and we were obviously attracted to each other, but was it only sex on his part? He has never mentioned the incident again, and has been polite and gentlemanly since then, but I cannot forget it."

"How awful. He seems so nice. Perhaps it is the effect of being too long in the sun. What are you going to do?"

"Well, we're in this play together, whatever, so I'll see how that pans out. I so hate what happened. I really thought at one moment he might attempt to make love to me by force, and it disturbs me that I should think so."

"Ruth. He does not look like a rapist to me. Not that I'm an expert. I should try and erase that thought from your mind and just think of him as an apparently nice man with so much male chauvinism in his make-up that he hardly saw how bad his behaviour was. I bet he spent a lot of time abroad in the company of men only. Polo, pig sticking and drunken curry parties."

She smiled at this and bought me another glass of that vinegary wine.

"Not sure there is too much pig sticking these days in an Independent Nigeria."

I felt so sorry for Ruth. It was just possible that Jeremy was shaping up, in her eyes, as a candidate for 'Mr Right' and so for this to have happened was such a disappointment. I wondered if there was anything I could do to help, but what? I could try confronting Jeremy and render him ashamed of his conduct by a speech of such withering scorn he would lower his eyes at my tone and collapse into a state of utter contrition. Absurd. I was as incapable of making such a statement as I was of playing Desdemona, and even if I did manage to utter a word or two of condemnation, he would ignore me, as he usually does, or walk away. When I next came across George strolling down the High Street wreathed in pipe smoke, I told him of my dilemma.

In addition to the revelation about Jeremy, there was one further incident that arose from the first read-through. Although he had accepted the disturbance caused by Tone, I knew Ambrose was furious at the interruption. I can recall at the Dress Rehearsal of an earlier production, when I was in the properties team, he had given evidence that the jumps might soon begin just because the mild-mannered Reg had sneezed loudly while sitting at the rear of the hall, waiting patiently to escort me home in Matilda.

But now he is reluctant to take action as a result of Tone because of the delicate balance between the role of Alison, as performer, and at the same time as his Lolita. Ignore my exaggeration. Ambrose is not a Humbert Humbert, and never will be, but you can understand there is a dichotomy between the attraction she is in his eyes, however unrewarding that is likely to be, and the thespian spirit that wants to prove his choice can fill the role of Sibyl: a contest between the sight of her shapely form on stage and the theatrical blood that courses so strongly through his veins.

Once again he turned to me.

"May, my dear. Do you know if Alison and that odious Hells Angel are likely to have a long-term relationship?"

"I have no idea."

"I rather hope not. He is, in my opinion, a bad influence. She is much too good for him. But, what cannot be denied is that if he repeats that disgraceful performance of the other night my rehearsals are going to be badly affected. It will not do. I cannot have it."

"I agree. Why don't you have a word with her and instruct her to keep the boy away until rehearsals are over. Or stay outside."

"Instruct. I cannot do that. She is a highly strung artiste. Must be handled carefully."

Yes, you would like that I thought.

"So, what's to be done?"

"Could I ask you to have a word. Try and get her to give him the push for her own good and the good of the Players."

For a moment I thought he was going to add that I might seduce him away from her but even Ambrose did not have the cheek to suggest that, nor even the imagination to believe such an action was a possibility.

"She won't listen to me. We hardly know each other. She is not a member of the tennis club, nor is she a fan of books."

I could see he did not understand the reference to tennis or literature.

"I'm sure she will. She looks on you as one of her favourite aunties."

So gallant, is he not. Nevertheless I told him I would have a word with her, but deliberately failed to do so. Not that it mattered. I was, in passing, mildly thanked by Ambrose when Tone's absence was noted – but only because Alison had moved on to a chap who worked in a pub and who was not available to be her chauffeur until after closing time.

I told my mother we were back in France and would not be taking this production of the Great Selsdon Amateur Dramatic Society on a tour of East Anglia. When Ambrose had first talked of Great Yarmouth I had suggested to George that this would be a great excuse for taking one of our plays for a performance, or performances, away from home territory. For a moment he took my idea seriously and began to consider how we would transport the set. He really is gullible, but harmless, which is more than can be said for Roger who is, however, not his usual evil confident self. Well again, I perhaps overstate the case with the word 'evil' – but something is wrong. I now know why Ruth and Jeremy are at odds with one another but where does that leave us? From previous experience, productions tend to run more smoothly – or at least less chaotically – if the cast is relatively tolerant of each other, but already we seem to have Ruth antagonistic towards Jeremy, Jeremy dismissive of Ambrose, Ambrose besotted with the doubtful Alison and Roger, if nothing else, angry with Ruth on behalf of Brenda.

Mon dieu, as Louise would say.

Chapter Four

The Cast and the Play

BEFORE WE embark on the sometime stormy passage of rehearsals for this play, I will provide some background information on the dramatis personae, and the members of the Society representing these characters, together with a résumé of the story – limited as it is.

SIBYL. She is very pretty and blonde, and smartly dressed in travelling clothes.

I commented to Eric that the famous tantrums of our red-headed Director were not up to his usual standard but as Sibyl, in the shapely form of Alison Street, refused to appear, he began to find some of his customary fury. Alison was of course one of the reasons why Ambrose was not firing on all cylinders. He would not admit it to us – or probably even to himself – that he had made a mistake. Or had he? She was decorative and sweet and had the loveliest of dimples so if some ability with words, and an improvement over the gauche way she moved could be added, it might prove to be not such a bad choice after all.

In my chronicle to-date I have rather mocked this girl but to be fair she was a member of the Society because she liked being on stage sparkling away, for four nights only, to three hundred of her fellow citizens. Up to now she had been able to achieve this goal as a member of the chorus in *Puss-in-Boots*, a Covent Garden bystander

61

in *Pygmalion* and climaxing with her triumph as Dorothy. She had applied for the part of Gwendoline in Wilde's masterpiece but when she asked Ambrose if she could cut out the line about the diary providing sensational reading when travelling by train, she could not understand what it meant, Ambrose had rightly chosen elsewhere and suggested, *sotto voce,* that she might look for stardom as the principal boy in Cinderella. As you can see, his infatuation at that time was very much in its infancy.

Again, am I being reasonable? Infatuated yes, but I think we must give him the benefit of the doubt and suggest that he saw the potential to convert this beautiful, but apparently talentless creature, into a Sibyl.

Was there a beauty and the beast myth in this production, if Ambrose can be described as beastly? Being with Alison made him feel good. He knew that he was never going to be involved in any real intimacy with this girl but he enjoyed taking her by the shoulders and showing where she should stand and giving her a hug and a kiss on the cheek when she managed to complete a dozen lines, error-free and in order. She did not mind. She could see it was only a game and she knew how it was played.

After a particularly dire performance by Alison at one of the early rehearsals he asked me to stay behind when the other three had gone. Alison had left by 9.30. Things were certainly changing. In the past Ambrose had been nearly as oblivious to my existence as Trevor, or Roger, but something seems to have changed. Timidity is still a strong feature of my personality but occasionally I raise my eyes from the ground when Ambrose wants some errand performed. I have always secretly been rather fond of the man. He has the best interests of the Society at heart, even if being vainglorious is an equally strong motive, but was he so frustrated with Alison he was going to make an amorous advance towards me? Should I begin our meeting with, 'Ambrose, alone at last.'? Of course I did not.

"What's the problem?"

"We can all see Alison is struggling."

"Yes, you could say that."

"I thought I should find time for some personal coaching."

"Good idea."

"Could you ask her to come round to the shop at closing time and I will spend an hour or two with her."

I quietly suggested her current boyfriend, or boyfriends, might not like that but then, with a confidence never displayed before, I went further.

"Ambrose. I think that would be unwise. Wagging tongues – and so on. You realise people in the Society are saying that you only chose her because of her brilliant blue eyes and shapely legs, even if they are rarely seen. She always seems to be wearing trousers."

"Nonsense."

"Is it? Be honest. Millicent read the part well at the auditions but you only have eyes for one. Now, tell the truth."

"I say again, nonsense. I agree, Millicent is the better actress. But this is Coward. Beautiful people. Beautiful young things and Alison fills that criterion."

"Yes. If you can work your magic, but not after-hours at Pottingers. May I make a suggestion?"

"Of course."

"Let me have a word with her. Tell her that with the stellar cast you have assembled this is going to be one of our greatest hits but if she does not concentrate, Millicent and not she will be part of that triumph. I might even suggest she gives up some of that busy social life of hers to make sure she is there at the end. Tell her you have total faith in her and if she follows your direction carefully she will be wonderful."

"Splendid. What a lieutenant you are proving to be."

Private Lives impacted on some of our own private lives which is, of course, the subject of my little tale. In more or less every case, external influences move the directions we take, for good or evil. Being in the right place at the right time is so often quoted but there are many other incidents to consider. The chance meeting; across a crowded room; a close encounter on a packed tube train or prosaically, 'we met at a party'. The school you attend; the teacher you have; your parents; the eccentric maiden aunt; something someone says that you never forget. Arbitrary items although critical, essential, and vital in your growth, but it is my contention that the world of amateur dramatics can provide more influences, diversions and coincidences than in decades of the normal course of human endeavour.

And, as can be observed, in my case it is happening already. See how bold I am becoming.

Not that my words transformed Alison into a Felicity Kendal, but I think she took to heart my comments about being part of a sell-out success – next stop Broadway – so she began to listen a little more attentively to Ambrose's instructions. One instance. Unless the rehearsal method is familiar to you, most will not appreciate how the process of the Director coaxing and teasing out a performance works. Or is supposed to work. Converting Alison into a semblance of a Sibyl was a very typical, if difficult, example. From Act One.

ELYOT:*I'm not doing anything. I'm only asking you, imploring you to come away from this place.*
SIBYL:*But I love it here.*
ELYOT:*There are thousands of other places far nicer.*
SIBYL:*It's a pity we didn't go to one of them.*
ELYOT:*Now, listen, Sibyl –*
SIBYL:*Yes, but why are you behaving like this, why, why, why?*
ELYOT:*Don't ask why. Just give in to me. I swear I'll never ask you to give into me over anything again.*
SIBYL [with complete decision]: *I won't think of going tonight. It is utterly ridiculous. I have done quite enough travelling for one day, and I'm tired.*
ELYOT:*You are as obstinate as a mule.*
SIBYL:*I like that, I must say.*
ELYOT [hotly]: *You've got your nasty little feet dug into the ground, and you don't intend to budge an inch, do you?*
SIBYL:*No, I do not.*
ELYOT:*If there's one thing in the world that infuriates me, it's sheer wanton stubbornness. I should like to cut off your head with a meat axe.*
SIBYL:*How dare you talk to me like that, on our honeymoon night.*
ELYOT:*Damn our honeymoon night. Damn it, damn it, damn it.*
SIBYL [bursting into tears]: *Oh, Elli. Elli –*
ELYOT:*Stop crying. Will you or will you not come away with me to Paris?*

SIBYL:I've never been so miserable in my life. You're hateful and beastly. Mother was perfectly right. She said you had shifty eyes.

"Alison. You are doing well tonight, trying much harder, but Sibyl changes at this point. We can try and make it more light hearted and fluffy earlier on. You do know there is not a lot of seriousness in this masterpiece but now you have to appear to be strong. A little stamp of the foot."

"On Roger's toes?"

"No, my precious, on the stage. Think about it. You and your new husband are on your honeymoon in Blackpool and as soon as you arrive at the glamorous hotel where you are to spend your first night together – you pair of innocents – quite suddenly he insists you leave at once and return to Great Selsdon. To your mother. You wouldn't agree, would you?"

"Not bloody likely."

"Alison, we are not doing *Pygmalion*. Anger, not blasphemy. See what I mean? You have to show Elyot that he cannot always have his own way. A trace of steel, my dear. Some resistance. A metaphorical stamping of the foot."

Alison was about to begin jumping up and down on the spot but she must have seen some of the steel in Ambrose so refrained and carried on.

He was beginning to achieve some variation between the joyful Sibyl who, at the beginning of the Act, declares, 'Oh dear, I'm so happy' and then later on says that she has never been so miserable in all her life. But, beside distinctions of tone, there are three other essential ingredients in a theatrical performance, movement, diction and articulation. Alison could be shrill enough when she wanted to – generally when she did not get her own way – but that ability did not necessarily enable her to project her voice to the back of the hall.

As I have said, this was not the Palladium but every attempt is made to ensure that the theatregoer sitting on the back row can distinguish what is being said on stage. We do not always succeed. I recall one of the Bank's customers who was cashing a cheque at my station saying that he had been seated at the rear of our auditorium the previous night and asked a question about the performance.

"I thought it was *The Importance of being Ernest* but in the first act I could not hear what Algy was saying and I began to wonder if I was seeing the Wilde play or some other Edwardian comedy."

I sympathised. George Robertson had not been the first choice for Algernon Moncrieff; he really should have been restricted to the hammer and the nails. There were similar complaints at Dobson Antiques where he was the auctioneer. If the porter did not hold up high the chair you thought you were bidding for, you would not know from George what lot had been reached. Perhaps he should have been the porter and not occupying the rostrum at Dobsons, or the stage with the Players, roles that required his strangled speech to be heard closer than a few feet away.

Ambrose had therefore to get Alison to pronounce her vowels and consonants with the precise clipped tone of the English upper classes, but in sufficient volume to fill the hall with her words.

Don't laugh at me, you mustn't be blasé about honeymoons just because this is your second.

"No, Alison. Again. Try emphasising the letter 'b'. Blasé and because."

She tries again.

"Good. But I am now going to move to the back of the hall. Say it again."

Repeat.

"Sibyl. I cannot hear you."

It got better, but persuading her to move quickly and gracefully was more difficult. Ambrose knew this was going to be a problem so he gave me another task.

"We are lucky that Doreen has agreed to do the costumes again. What would we do without her? I had such a lovely meeting on Thursday looking at 1920s fashion but now I see how difficult Alison is finding it to trip about the stage like a gazelle, I believe the quicker we get her into costume, and the right shoes, the more chance there is of getting it right on the night."

Right on the night. How often that phrase slips out in the amateur theatrical world; but perhaps it does at the National as well. It stands in partnership with what is said after a disastrous Dress Rehearsal.

Not to worry; it'll be all right on the night. What happens if the first performance is a matinee?

"Could you ask Doreen if we could have a tight garment, a rehearsal dress not fully finished, that we can confine Sibyl into now – and place shoes on her feet – with heels."

Alison must have worn a dress during her short life, but even for her Saturday night date I suspect her attire differed little from the norm; trainers, jeans and a low-cut top and so I thought Ambrose's idea was an excellent one. Doreen came up trumps. It was a deep blue sheath that fitted closely from her neck to well below the knee and even managed to flatten out her prominent bosom. The heels of the shoes were about three inches high with straps across the instep and Ambrose added a long string of pearls, said to have belonged to his Grandmother. They were certainly old; very discoloured.

The next rehearsal, when our young heroine was so attired, was an unmitigated disaster. At one stage we thought another Sibyl would need to be found when Alison tottered about and actually fell off the stage on to Roger, who was hunched up in the body of the kirk trying to keep warm. The nights were getting colder and the Hall heating was not switched on until the first of October. She complained of a broken leg and he grumbled that he thought this was supposed to be a piece of drama and not a circus. He wanted to know when the clowns were due to appear, insinuating that with Ambrose's Sibyl one of them had arrived already.

But, again, she improved. It was the shoes that were the answer; they seemed to give her poise. I thought all women liked shoes but such a passion seemed to have passed Alison by. Nevertheless, she soon began to admire herself raised a few inches above the ground and I am sure that one evening, a week or two later, I caught sight of her crossing the High Street wearing a skirt.

All of these difficulties could be overcome if there was some talent in the pupil – however minimal – and some skill in the teacher, but what Ambrose could not do was to learn the words for her. For most amateurs this either comes easily, or is very difficult. I am in the latter category. Because the few parts I have had were so minor I could achieve total blackout over just a word or two and, even more worrying, forget completely the cue line that would allow me to insert, 'Anyone for tennis'. My experience is that those with the major parts learn their lines more proficiently than those with very few. This was certainly true of Roger. He was word perfect at a very early stage but his problem was that in his confidence he often added words of his own, or presented the playwright's language exactly as written, but not necessarily in the right order.

I must say Alison persevered. When Amanda and Elyot were occupying the stage, I would act as Victor, or her new husband, and have her say her lines. Very hard work. She missed out whole sentences but did not have Roger's aplomb and supreme self-confidence to plough on. Ambrose became angrier and angrier as his protégée interspersed her part with 'Damn' or 'Bugger' or 'That's wrong isn't it.'

As I drove her home one night she was close to tears.

"You seem down in the dumps tonight, Alison. What's the matter?"

"Nothing."

"Yes, there is. You're usually so composed."

"I don't know what it is. Think I'm fed up with Sibyl. Are they real these people? I know I'm not exactly a level-headed, hard-working member of the society; church on Sunday, good works, love my neighbour, and all that, but Coward's people believe in nothing. They do nothing. They make no contribution to humanity."

Was this Alison Street: the pretty empty-headed dumb blonde – object of the affection of most of the male population of Great Selsdon? Indeed, my mother tells me that even Eric whistles when she walks by his shop. Was an exposure to Coward's *Private Lives* already beginning to reveal another side to this girl that no one realised existed?

"That's true. There's a line in Act Two where Amanda says something about her beliefs. Being kind, giving money to old beggar women and being as gay as can be; but, Alison, it's not about who they are, or what they say. It's about love. It might be a strange form of love but it's a comedy about how all-consuming love is. How strong it can be for these two people. In the 1920s and 1930s there might have been a small coterie of wealthy folk who acted like that, spoke like that – selfish and narrow minded – but that's not the point. It's mainly funny because they are like that. If they talked about the threat of communism and the yellow peril, or debated the relative merits of Turner and Manet, it would be a different play – as it would be if they were hungry or suffering from cancer."

Alison was listening intently.

"Of course, they could be the poor working class and just as much in or out of love – take *Love on the Dole* for instance – but it would not be the same. It would not be Coward. In his *Hay Fever* a family, parents and two children, have visitors to their house over one weekend. All four begin haphazard love affairs with the others but it all comes to nothing and at the end of the play the spurned leave, unnoticed by the family who are arguing amongst themselves. See what I mean. Coward. Sound familiar?"

"Gosh May. I have never heard such a long speech from you before. You know a lot don't you."

"Well, I don't know about that, but I'm interested in how the theatre – good theatre – can add another dimension to our lives. I think they said about Noël Coward that he had 'a talent to amuse'. He used it in another of his songs. 'But I believe that since my life began/ The most I've had is just a talent to amuse.' You should look at it like that. We are going to amuse our audience and you will be a winner."

At the next rehearsal Alison came and put her arm around me and said she had given up her latest boyfriend and could I lend her a copy of *Hay Fever*. It was a turning point in her attempt to play Sibyl and except for her inability to remember all the words, she delivered most of them in a manner the Master would have approved of. The problem was not that she missed a line or two on each of the four nights of the run; the real mischief was that at each performance the omissions were different, which only enraged the others. As for Ambrose, he thought these variations added to the charm.

ELYOT. He is about thirty, quite slim and pleasant looking and also in travelling clothes.

Although in the matter of age Roger did not comply with this description, he is nearly fifty, he is probably the only member of the Society who could have been cast in this part. He is slim, still had all of his hair and, I must admit, is moderately good looking. He carried himself well and was sufficiently athletic to make a credible job of the difficult scene at the end of Act Two where he and Amanda are physically at each other's throats. All Directors had an easy task with Roger, provided he was cast in character and in one of the principal parts, except for one problem and that was his total oblivion to everyone else on stage. I do not mean that he did not interact with the other characters, of course he did, and he was expert in getting the tone of his replies and interjections absolutely right; an essential in this play. What I am trying to say is that he did not help them. If Amanda or Sibyl or even Victor did not respond to an Elyot line instantly, Roger was into his next one before they had time to react. He out-shone everyone on stage through his ability and his arrogance but the prejudiced me questioned whether this was good for our *Private Lives* as a whole.

Ruth rebelled. She refused to lie down and be 'Rogered' as she described it to me. Normally it was Brenda who was subjected to this treatment but with her professional training, and her temperament, she was his equal. This meant that when they were the two principals, Roger's overbearing self-importance was not so noticeable but with another leading lady, it distorted what was happening on stage. Ambrose tried to erase, or level this out, but he had a difficult task. When the Director tried to point out these problems to Roger, our Donald Wolfit nodded his head, but as to tamping down his bravura routine, not a chance. There was one passage in particular where, at an early rehearsal, Ambrose was rendered speechless.

AMANDA: Yes. What fools we were to ruin it all. What utter, utter fools.
ELYOT: You feel like that too, do you?
AMANDA [wearily]: Of course.
ELYOT: Why did we?
AMANDA: The whole business was too much for us.
ELYOT: We were so ridiculously over in love.
AMANDA: Funny, wasn't it?
ELYOT [sadly]: Horribly funny.
AMANDA: Selfishness, cruelty, hatred, possessiveness, petty jealousy.
All those qualities came out in us just because we loved each other.

After 'You feel like that too, do you?', Amanda was cut out of the exchange until 'Selfishness' etc, and only then because, as per the stage instructions, Elyot's line before that was to be delivered 'sadly'.

'Roger. We all know the dialogue, particularly between Elyot and Amanda, has to be quick-fire but you are shooting Ruth down in flames. If you do not recognize the full stop after, 'You feel like that too, do you.' Ruth will not be able to respond, wearily or any other way. May I suggest you take a breath at the end of each of your lines?'

Roger was furious at this and I could see he was about to blame Ruth because she did not respond rapidly enough but then thought better of it, even though he could not resist a little dig.

"Will do Ambrose, but we must not go too slowly. Perhaps Amanda should stand closer to me and then the lines will bounce backwards and forwards more effectively."

Ruth shrugged her shoulders at this as if she did not want to even be on the same stage as Roger, never mind in a clinch. Except that is for the fight scene which, as I shall recount, she enjoyed immensely

His superiority, of ability and manner, came even more to the fore when paired with Alison. As written, Sibyl does not have the same strong character as Amanda. She is younger and less sophisticated, but she does have to show some backbone, some spirit, in resisting Elyot and when quarrelling with Victor at the end of the play. Jeremy was able to bring this out in Alison in their final scene together but as soon as Roger was the counterpart, her inexperience and naivety were fully exposed. He was not prepared to make any sacrifices to help the girl; as far as he was concerned Ambrose had chosen her and why should he tone down his acting because of that mistake. At one stage I thought this problem was going to seriously affect the success of the play. Alison could be coached up the scale but could Ambrose soften Roger enough for there to be a meeting halfway?

I could see the crux of the difficulty: who had the stronger character, the Director or the leading man? I suppose it did not arise with Donald Wolfit because he was both but in our case we had a Director with his hands so filled with the task of transforming his protégé thistle into an English rose he found it difficult to counteract the single-mindedness of Roger. Even without the Alison problem, he and Roger were mismatched. I hesitate to suggest there was a distinction in class, shopkeeper and solicitor, but their personalities were very different. Roger was taciturn but determined and Ambrose loquacious and, despite the tantrums that were outside of his control, easy-going and charming. I assume Brenda saw similar qualities in her own husband, but I doubt if many other people did. On the other hand, this comment only goes to illustrate what a good actor he is. Elyot may be unreliable, lazy and thoughtless but no one can deny the charm: he is one of the most charming Prince Charmings of British Theatre and the unlikable Roger assumed this mantle as easily and effortlessly as shelling peas.

I wondered what had been the outcome of the Ambrose versus Roger contest in previous plays. We would not have had a semi-permanent Director and an invariable leading man unless the partnership had worked in the past, but then I realised the difference now was the absence of Brenda. That was certainly part of the answer because I could envisage that when they were on stage together, Brenda was able, in many subtle ways, to persuade her husband to adjust his performance. There was another reason why Ambrose did not seem able to restrain Roger. Despite the Director's easygoing manner they were clearly, during this production, not the best of friends for reasons, so I discovered, outside of our little theatrical world.

Whatever the cause, my support went to Ambrose in this contest, but I was not too confident. What I was sure of was that if total victory was gained by Roger, the potential success of this production might well be jeopardised. Strangely, Ambrose did not seem to worry. Did he not see the problem or did he have up his sleeve another way of solving it? Was there a master plan, a scheme to bring Roger crashing to earth? Is there a second strand to the Great Yarmouth plot: Elyot in a wheelchair perhaps? A picture comes to mind of a supine Roger Scotland, with Ambrose holding aloft his copy of the script while one of his highly polished shoes rests triumphantly on the head of the defeated. Well, we can all dream, can we not; but we shall see.

VICTOR. He is quite nice looking, about thirty or thirty-five. He is dressed in a light travelling suit.

When we see Victor and Amanda together on the terrace he has the line, 'I'm glad I'm normal.' I think Ambrose took that at its face value and decided Victor should be portrayed as the only stable member of the quartet, particularly as a contrast to the mad idiosyncrasies of his new wife and Elyot. This was probably an accurate interpretation but I thought such a conclusion was not altogether correct – more complexities than superficially appear. Jeremy also saw something more than the square-jawed, solid, middle-aged, well-mannered gentleman and I could see he tried to add some touches of his own.

If we crossed Siberia by train we could be in China in a fortnight, but I don't see any reason to do it.

The tone of sarcasm used to deliver that line was clearly evident and with that, and other examples, he filled out the role with some skill. I learned later he was familiar with the play having been cast as Elyot in a production in Lagos. I can only conjecture how this very English of artefacts went down in the tropics but he told us that many of their audience of expatriates were more conservative and right-wing than you would find today in the UK, even in Cheltenham. Were they also, I wondered, as frivolous as Coward's creations?

And what was a 'light travelling suit'? Do we have such suits today?

Jeremy was sufficiently experienced that just after Alison began to wear a 1920s dress and high heel shoes at the rehearsal, he also began to appear wearing a rather shiny three-piece suit and brown suede shoes. He called it his 'country gear', but I speculated that it had probably been handed down by his father. For the actual performance, Doreen came up with something in keeping with the tailoring of the day but in rather better condition than the tweeds he wore at rehearsals. Nevertheless, this effort to dress the part so early in the process was an indication of his interest in being involved in this play, and in the Players generally.

It would also appear that he was beginning to grow a moustache: Victor's upper lip would surely have been so adorned.

He was below average height, perhaps he could even be described as dapper. Except for a twisted nose, rugby accident he said, he was handsome of face and as graceful as a Rudolph; Nureyev that is, not the reindeer. He had a rather attractive cleft in his chin but was not robust enough to resemble Kirk Douglas. Jeremy's hair was naturally wavy: it spread across his head like the ripples on a gentle sea. It was dark in colour, not a hint of grey. Was it dyed I wondered? Grecian something or other? I assumed he was in his early fifties. As to personality, he did not exhibit the superior manner of a Roger, but I suspect if aroused he could be even more sarcastic and supercilious than our leading man, but he kept such traits well under control. He was a controlled man. His hair was not long enough to be let down but even if it was we rarely witnessed any spontaneity. He smiled at Ambrose's jokes but there was never any evidence that he was prepared to relax sufficiently to split his sides.

He was intelligent. When we did converse together, not very often, I discovered he was just as knowledgeable about the theatre as I was and I think we had in common a desire to see the Society engaged in more adventurous works. That is the only thing we had in common. I was barely half his age and a bank clerk: he was a Chartered Accountant. On one occasion I had the temerity to suggest that if he had time on his hands he might look at the Open University, particularly the Shakespeare unit they offered and that I had so enjoyed two years ago. He did manage to respond, but in a dismissive manner. He evidently filled his waking hours without needing advice from me; he was an enthusiastic member of the West Park Golf Club and his pension, and savings, allowed him to live in some style. He drove a Jaguar motorcar and was said, to be accumulating a considerable cellar of claret at Regency House, a Victorian property he had bought when first arriving at Great Selsdon.

Ambrose was delighted with Jeremy. Kept saying to me he had made the right choice but something was missing. He was too clinical. There was no warmth, and little signs of friendliness or comradeship with his fellow actors. He obviously recognized Roger's ability, although there seemed little love lost between them, but an antipathy towards Roger was not unusual. What was much more crucial was the relationship with Ruth that was really souring proceedings. He was clearly trying his best to win back her favour but in view of that evening together she was finding it difficult to accept this. She did not like Roger but her former pleasure at Jeremy's company had now swung towards a form of bitter disappointment. The lack of warmth in him that I saw did not help and although he was not as aloof and unpleasant as Roger, the behaviour of our two leading men did not exactly make rehearsals a fun-filled event. Oh for Owen Ready, I thought.

AMANDA. She is quite exquisite with a gay face and a perfect figure.

This is the best part in the play. Elyot has some of the funniest lines but as the rehearsals progressed it seemed to me that Amanda was the more human, the more genuine of this artificial couple and Ruth soon began to emphasise this. Elyot is very glib and rather camp but Roger's portrait was, in my view, not affectionate enough. This may just be my prejudice but I think Ambrose noticed it and on occasions I could see a smile of satisfaction spread across his face as Ruth appeared to turn the tables on our star performer. She was his choice and she did not let him down.

At first these were infrequent and only minor triumphs; Roger was too able and experienced – and conceited – to allow a relative newcomer to outshine him, but Ruth stuck to her task and when she succeeded, Ambrose really chuckled. He seemed able to utter this as though equal to a round of applause, and this did nothing to ease Roger's annoyance.

Let me give you one example. Early in Act Two she asks Elyot if he had ever crossed the Sahara on a camel, to which he replies:

Frequently. When I was a boy we used to do it all the time. My grandmother had a lovely seat on a camel.

Amanda's response is:

There's no doubt about it, foreign travel's the thing.

but before delivering the line, Ruth screwed up her face and nearly put out a tongue to indicate how foolish, nay stupid, was Elyot to come up with such a glib response. This was followed up by the line itself, spoken in such a way as to reinforce her facial expression. Roger was fazed, a thing that had not happened many times in his acting career – and Ambrose was in raptures. And so was I.

These differences were only obvious to the trained observer and neither Ambrose, Roger or Ruth would have wanted them to be seen during the public performances, but then, this is what this little story is all about – the raw ingredients that made up the final product that is presented to the paying public. Our *Noises Off* may not have been as loud or hysterical as those in the Michael Frayn play, but they were there nevertheless.

Where Ambrose did need to make a contribution was in the requirement to render Ruth more forceful, and he achieved this with remarkable success. She was mostly withdrawn in her own persona and realised that she had to over-ride this to portray the sophisticated Amanda, a woman who can stand next to Mr Coward's Elyot and outshine him. Not everyone sees it that way but in my opinion Elyot is, eventually, not the dominant one. They are joint partners in the final escape, leaving Victor and Sibyl quarrelling, but Amanda deals with the contradictions in the last Act with more aplomb and humour than does Elyot and in due course Ruth managed to show this. That she did so in opposition to the quick-fire retorts of Roger only goes to reveal her hidden strength. She was to become the victorious Amanda of our *Private Lives*, both on and off the stage.

LOUISE She is rather frowsy-looking girl …..

The maid has six lines to utter at the beginning of Act Three, all spoken in French. My intuition told me that instead of a move to Great Yarmouth, the one change Ambrose might contemplate is to cut out Louise altogether. She is hardly germane to the antics of the fabulous four.

That is our cast but before we go any further I will give you the plot of *Private Lives*, if not already over-familiar. Plot? There is not much of that. Elyot and Sibyl are on their honeymoon staying at a hotel in Deauville. He has been married before, to Amanda, who has also just re-married, to Victor, and they are spending their honeymoon in the room adjoining the other couple at the same hotel.

Elyot and Amanda surprise each other as they meet on the adjoining terraces outside the rooms. Elyot tries to persuade Sibyl they should leave at once and Amanda similarly pleads with her new husband. Neither spouse will agree and Amanda and Elyot find themselves alone on one of those fortunate terraces and then run away together to Paris. End of Act One.

Acts Two and Three take place in the sitting room of a Paris flat. In the first Elyot and Amanda have just finished dinner. Initially they are blissfully happy as they chatter away but this turns to bickering, then a real quarrel and finally they fight each other, physically. During the ensuing wrestling match they trip over a piece of carpet and as they are both prone, Victor and Sibyl enter. The newcomers are ignored by the pugilists as they exit left and right, slamming doors as Victor and Sibyl move further into the room and sit on the sofa. The next morning, in Act Three, all four squabble with allegiances moving about like a jelly on a plate, but as the play comes to an end, the serious quarrel settles itself as a fight between Sibyl and Victor and while this is at its height, the other two silently depart with smiles on their faces.

The play was first performed in London on the 8th of September 1930 with the author playing Elyot, Gertrude Lawrence as Amanda, Laurence Olivier Victor and Adrianne Allen as Sibyl.

Chapter Five

The Stage Crew – and others

DRAMA REQUIRES the audience to accept two things. Firstly, the guy who lives next door by the name of Bert, who works as an insurance salesman and is as passionate as a cold cup of tea is, before your very eyes, transformed into Romeo and secondly, this role-playing is taking place not on the stage at the Village Hall because we need to show Bert, the actor, in the proper setting for his performance; Verona for Romeo or Venice for Shylock or New Orleans for Stanley Kowalski. Well, most always. Much of Samuel Beckett's work can be performed in neutral territory but with *Private Lives*, specific is specific, whether it is France or the North Sea coast of Britain. As a result, on our stage we had to provide, in Act One, two adjoining hotel terraces and for the remainder of the play, an interior complete with a piano – preferably a Steinway Grand.

The first Act is a long one but even so at its end we are by no means halfway through the play; twenty eight pages in my copy of the script out of a total of sixty seven, but the Interval has to come before we start page twenty nine so that the set can be changed.

On the limited stage we have at our disposal alterations to the set are often difficult. In *Separate Tables* the action moves backwards and forwards from the dining room to the lounge at the Beauregard Hotel so often that we could only signify the difference by bringing on, and taking off, a number of dining tables. Very tricky because some of these transformations had to be undertaken behind closed curtains with the audience still in place; we could hardly have five intervals. I will not bore with the fiasco this proved to be on the first two nights as stagehands collided with each other. Beryl nearly suffered some serious damage to her left eye, inflicted by a roving table leg, but even so, this was as nothing compared with the problems with *Pygmalion*.

There are two interiors for this play, Higgins laboratory and his mother's drawing room, and we were able to distinguish one from the other by bringing on the Professor's instruments and moving around the furniture but Act One at Covent Garden was another matter altogether. It was Eric's fault. He was proud of the fact that he had been able to acquire a number of wooden cylinders that had been the core to some major electric cables and he used these to represent the columns at the portico of St Paul's Church. Painted grey they looked very authentic but when it came to moving them after that first short Act they were so heavy and cumbersome the stage staff could not make the change silently. In fact, on the first night Simon let go of the end he was carrying with a very painful result that brought forth a stream of expletives from Eric that could be heard throughout the auditorium. The big toe on his right foot quickly swelled up to resemble one of his superior sausages.

Intervals are also essential for other reasons. I do not suppose Great Selsdon is different from other communities but we have discovered that our mature audience cannot sit for two hours without enjoying what cricket commentators these days refer to as a 'comfort break'. Why a visit to the lavatory should be more comfortable for a Dennis Compton than anyone else, I do not know. Incidentally, do you notice the wicketkeeper has to bide his time; no substitute for him. I have never watched a serious game of cricket played by ladies. Do they leave the room more often than the men?

But I digress. In addition to the needs of nature, we look to the Interval bar sales to add some extra to the play's proceeds; and it is also a splendid opportunity, for those who are so inclined, to listen to some of the comments being made about the first half, if the audience talk about the play at all. In my experience most of the clientele use the gap between the chatter on stage, after making themselves comfortable, to continue the conversation or argument they had on the way to the venue. Sometimes this is mixed with the occasional, 'I could do better than that Mabel Sykes. Couldn't hear a word she said.' Or, 'They had better not slam that door too hard. It's about to come off its hinges.' Sadly though it was more often, 'Where are you going for your holidays this year?' or, 'No, there is not time for another one. In any case, you had more than your fair share last night and I had to clean up the mess.'

You would have thought that after watching an hour or so of live theatre the urgent topic of conversation would be the play we had sweated over for the last three months, but not so. I see this as a very ungrateful response. We have given up our spare time for weeks and weeks which are ignored as Horace flirts with a stranger's wife or the men consider the chances of Aston Villa proceeding to the next round of the FA cup.

Nevertheless, fixing the Interval was the least of Ambrose's worries: his major concern was where do we get the Steinway from, and who is to play it? The pianist, rather than the instrument, turned out to be a fairly minor problem. Roger told Ambrose at the read-through that he was sure he could manage to coax a few notes from the keyboard and that he had spoken to Vera about a spot of coaching in the 'singing of a song' department. I was surprised at the reference to Vera. Because of her former life many folk in the town thought she was Madam Showbiz and that she could kick up her heels like a Windmill Girl and croon like Dorothy Squires, but the days of the kicking up of legs were well over. On the other hand, she always coped with the music in the pantomimes very well but what did amaze me was that Roger would even deign to recognize her existence. He was obviously pulling out all the stops. It was clearly his intention that this portrayal of Elyot Chase was to be the *pièce de résistance* of his theatrical career to date, spurred on I thought because Ambrose had not voted him the part without question – or included Brenda.

The ego is the most extraordinary of senses. Or, not to restrict it to that, the will we have to push ourselves beyond what we think our capacity is. Am I explaining myself well? Probably not. Van Gogh was not your average stable personality but he was driven, like his friend Gauguin, to give up everything to paint the visions he had in his brain. Where did Mother Teresa find that resilience in such a tiny frame? Why did Beethoven not call it a day when he became deaf? Now, I'm not suggesting that Roger is in any danger of joining such a pantheon of heroes, or heroines, but there is no doubt in my mind he is going the extra mile in his portrayal of Elyot beyond simply learning the lines and turning in his usual polished performance.

Or is this again an example of my exaggerated imagination? Is he just being Roger – as normal? But, consulting Vera! He will be selling all his worldly goods and giving them to the poor next. I am surprised he even knew of her existence; he had certainly kept well clear of the Yellow Brick Road. Vera was as surprised as I was but being who she is she got on with the job and bought a copy of the *Noel Coward Song Book* – and put it to good use, as we were to discover.

I can already hear the lilting sounds of *Someday I'll Find You*, and other sentimental melodies, floating over the footlights at the Village Hall and bringing tears to the eyes of many of the romantic in our audience. Provided, of course, there is a piano. I had already guessed that for a moment Ambrose was of a mind to solve this little difficulty by using a gramophone record but that would never do. This is Noël Coward. What image do we have of him? Immaculate evening clothes seated at a shiny black piano, cigarette in an ebony holder emitting smoke from the ashtray where it has been deposited by the Master as he sings *Poor Little Rich Girl* or *A Room with a View* – but this is not going to happen without a piano.

Just occasionally Ambrose feels the need to consult the Committee on some aspect or other. Not very often, but with *Private Lives* he asked me to speak to Trev and request him to call together the personnel that are supposed to constitute the engine room of the Great Selsdon Amateur Dramatic Society. Our Chairman had assumed that he would not be involved again until the exhilarating end-of-the-show party when he would be complimenting his troops on a well fought campaign, but I managed to persuade him that Ambrose needed his wise counsel now. He therefore graciously authorised me to call the gathering the Director had requested.

"Ambrose. Bit of a surprise this. You usually manage fine on your own. You certainly did with *The Winslow Boy*, if I recall."

"True Chairman. I did not even bother you when Professor Higgins caught bronchitis on the first night and had to mime his lines spoken from offstage by the prompt or when the property ladies lost the handbag that was to be shown to Lady Bracknell – but at this stage with Mr Coward, I have a bit of a technical teaser."

"Don't tell me your Alison, whatever her name is, has eloped?"

"No. No problems with the cast. Splendid crew. It's a piano."

"Piano? Didn't know we were doing *Salad Days*?"

Gosh, I thought, Trevor it is in good form tonight. Connecting a piano to *Salad Days* was an act of sheer genius; at least for an esteemed Chairman who had dismissed Albee's classic because he did not want a dangerous animal on the stage. Or was he mixing it up with something by Prokovief?

"No, Trevor. As you well know, we are not doing *Salad Days* but the leading man has to play the piano, crucial part of the interplay between him and his former wife. We are into romance, a love story, one of the most delightful in all theatre – and the piano is essential."

"Well, isn't there a piano at the Church Hall?"

As he made this statement of the blindingly obvious he looked at the Vicar but before the Rev Bob could respond, Ambrose, already becoming slightly hot under the collar, replied.

"Yes, but have you seen it. It is covered in mildew. Someone, at some time or other, has painted the top half a shade of green. It is incapable of being tuned. You can see the stains on the top from a generation or beer mugs. Even Madame Flora who teaches the Saturday morning ballet class now brings a record player, or one of her assistants plays the flute."

"Surely Am Am Am Ambrose, it's not that bad."

"You are lovely Bob, but it is. I cannot allow it to have any association whatsoever with Mr Coward. We need a Grand. A Steinway Grand."

"I see your point Ambrose old man, but where are you going to get one from?"

"Mr Chairman, for goodness sake, I don't know. That's why we are having a Committee Meeting."

"Well, we haven't got one, and even if we had, I doubt if Dorothy would be keen to lend it to you."

George ventured the thought that we could cover the shame of the existing instrument at the Hall with a black cloth. Tricia said would a guitar do as a substitute and Eric, attending in his capacity as Assistant Stage Manager, said he could make one out of hardboard. Ambrose's complexion was moving towards the Post Office van red I had used as a metaphor earlier so I tried to lower his temperature.

"Perhaps Ruth, through her teaching contacts, can see if there is a school nearby that has such an instrument they might lend us."

I could see the Chairman was about to crush me with a biting phrase indicating that I should be seen but not heard, except when reading out the minutes, but I found a surprising ally, Roger.

"That's the most sensible suggestion we have had yet. What about the Catholic girls school outside Evesham. Is it St Benedict's? They are as rich as Croesus. Nothing but the best for them. Do you know anyone there Vicar?"

This change of tack was helping Ambrose to regain his composure, but the effect on Bob was in the other direction.

"No. So so so sorry. Not part of us, you know."

Ambrose said he would ask Ruth to act as his emissary and he was about to indicate to Trev that the meeting could be brought to a close when Roger asked permission to raise a point.

"Ambrose. You and I have not always agreed in the past but I want to tell you that I think you are, by instinct, a very good Director and you always get the best out of us humble thespians."

Ambrose purred at this. He sounded like a large Persian cat.

"But, genius or not, I do believe you have taken on too difficult a task with Miss Street. Sibyl is not an Amanda, but it is a crucial part and she is not a vacant silly teenager, which in my view best describes your Alison."

There was a stress on the 'your'.

Ambrose vacillated. Talked about new talent and giving youth a chance. Pretty face. Stage presence. Give her time, but I could see he had taken Roger's comments to heart and so he promised to sleep on it. If sleep with it had been on the agenda, Roger would have been totally ignored, but as both Ambrose's age and the pick of Great Selsdon's eligible young men stood in the way of that possibility, another Sibyl was on the cards.

But, for now, the piano. Ruth came up trumps. Not exactly a Steinway, but it was not a green painted upright either. Trouble was it would not fit in the van of Eric the butcher, our usual source of free transport, but Helen arranged for the movement of the instrument to be undertaken by one of the transport companies to whom she was the printer. We had to pay £100 for the return journey, including unloading, but on arrival the gang was not prepared to add to their labours by positioning it where it was to be used and so, when we turned up for the rehearsal before the Dress one, the first task of actors and backstage staff was to manhandle that monster onto the stage. There were many complaints. Roger felt an urgent need to visit the lavatory, Eric pretended he had strained a wrist while cutting up some pork chops and Simon said he had not had any lunch that day and was feeling 'really buggered'. Brenda dealt with the matter. She bathed the gathered company in her radiant smile, rolled up the sleeves of the elegant sweater she was wearing and we all put our shoulders to the wheel.

The loan arranged with St Benedict's was for six days only so for the early rehearsals we had to manage with the green upright, still in the auditorium, but close to the stage. Elyot and Amanda are separated when he goes over to the piano. The stage instructions read as follows.

ELYOT looks at her, then goes over to the piano. He sits down and begins to play idly. AMANDA raises her head, screws herself around on the sofa, and lies there listening. Elyot blows a kiss to her and goes on playing. He starts to sing softly to her, never taking his eyes off her. When he has finished the little refrain, whatever it was, he still continues to play it looking at her.

Roger soon stopped proceedings.

"Even I know this thing is out of tune and there are three black notes near the middle that are dead. But how can I blow a kiss? I can't see her."

"Roger, my dear chap, could you not stand up a bit."

"While playing? I'll look like an idiot."

"But it's only for rehearsals. On the night, the Steinway will be on the stage."

"God willing. I know it's only a rehearsal but that's what rehearsals are for, to rehearse, precisely, what we will hopefully be doing on the night. You will have to get this piano on the stage."

"All right. I'll have a word with the Rev Bob."

Having a word with the Rev Bob was naturally delegated to me. He was not happy. Would it fall to pieces if removed from the spot where it has stood for the last twenty years. In any case, the Morris Dancers and the Glee Club need their music next to them at ground level. And where was the muscle to move it. The Vicar, so he told me, had strained his back at the baptism of the first set of triplets born in the town for many a long year, so he was *hors de combat.*

I took the initiative and asked Eric if he could arrange some of the stage hands to do the honours. He was sceptical, particularly when I explained that before the Dress Rehearsal the instrument needed to be back at floor level, preferably upright.

"Just because your mother is the best assistant I've ever had, that is no cause for you to get me all the nasty jobs."

"Eric dear. It's not me. Ambrose is worried Roger will walk out if the piano is not moved."

"Good, then I can be Elyot."

Was that the second grand plan; voluntary retirement by Roger after an argument over a piano? Not a hope, I thought. More at stake than a musical instrument.

"Be serious. I hate the guy, but at the moment he's the only thing going for this production. Alison is not paying attention and the other two seem to have fallen out, big time, and they make no effort to spark off each other."

"And moving that bloody piano is going to solve that?"

"Probably not, but one thing at a time. I'm really worried about Ambrose. He is not yet on form. Even his tantrums are second rate. Only eight weeks to go, and Roger and I are the only ones who know our lines."

"But you've only got about three. And they are in French, so big deal. Would you like one of my pork pies to cheer you up? Here, take one for Ambrose as well."

Our indefatigable ASM had the piano nestling near to the curtains before the next rehearsal but Ambrose refused the pork pie. Said he was trying to lose weight. Roger clapped him on the back, said well done, sat down at the instrument and played *Chopsticks* with great aplomb, but little musical ability. I was glad we were not doing *Salad Days*.

Compared to acquiring a suitable piano, the set was not too difficult. Brenda and Eric discussed with Ambrose how the transition from a pair of adjoining hotel terraces to a well furnished interior was to be achieved. We did not have enough depth of stage for Act One to be played in front of a screen concealing Amanda's apartment so Brenda devised a fairly neutral wall of flats that sufficed for both; it stretched all the way across the back of the stage. Instructions in the text called for French windows behind the terraces opening up into the two separate hotel suites but these windows had to be discarded due to the limited space available and so exits to the hotel rooms were made Stage Left and Right so they could also be used in Acts Two and Three. The two terraces were divided by a line of potted plants that were removed during the interval to be replaced by the furniture used for the interior action.

There were two added features, thanks to Brenda. A false window was wheeled on and placed against the back wall in the last two acts giving a view of the horse chestnut trees outside with an impression of the Sacre Cœur in the distance, and a device designed that enabled the piano to stay in place throughout the play. Everyone involved had made it quite clear that they were not prepared to move that massive instrument each night, on and off the stage and into the wings, and so Brenda had Eric construct a wooden casing that hid it from sight in Act One. It was a simple device. It had a low balustrade around the two sides on view to the audience and its top was littered with a variety of foliage planted in lightweight pots.

There was one minor mishap. Brenda decided that the neutral backdrop should be brightened up somewhat with a design of a fleur-de-lis pattern. She prepared a stencil so that the rear flats could be so decorated but Eric and his crew managed to apply this upside down. When she saw this she was considerably upset, but no one was prepared to start again and paint over the strange design that was now to grace our showing of *Private Lives*. Eric told my mother he thought it looked better than the other way round and in any case he thought a fleur-de-lis was the name of a French striptease artist.

Sam Troughton was usually in charge of lighting, as he was on this occasion. He was proficient but the board at our venue was very limited and this meant that lighting plots were necessarily simple. This was a continuous source of irritation for Ambrose. You would have thought by now he would be realistic and make do with what was available, but the conversation with Sam at the beginning of *Private Lives* was a duplicate of the ones at the start of each new play. With the pantomimes, Vera accepted the limitations and left the lighting man to get on with it, but Ambrose was like a dog worrying a bone that had already been licked clean.

"So glad you have agreed to do the lights again, my dear Sam, a load off my mind, I can tell you."

"Only too happy to oblige. Like doing it, provided we don't have a main fuse catch fire as we did with *Ring Round the Moon*."

"Don't mention it. Thank goodness Owen had a torch so at least we could open the bar. Now, for *Private Lives*, I want you to pull out all the stops."

"We'll do what the equipment will allow."

"Precisely. Now for Act One, I'll need separate spots for each terrace so we can emphasise the two acting areas."

"I think we can manage that."

"It's a summer evening, about eight o'clock, but by the end of the Act there is talk of a moon, so we need a gradual diminution of the overall lighting."

"More difficult, particularly with the spots. The dimmers on them are very limited."

"Can't we buy new ones?"

"Shouldn't think so. When last I asked was told, no money."

"Usual story. Silk purse. Sow's ear. I despair. Why do I do it?"

"Don't ask me."

"Sam. That was a rhetorical question, but to get on. The other two acts are simple. Both mornings, but I have an idea for a gradual lowering of the light level as Elyot moves to the piano and a gentle spot pinpoints him as he sings, *Someday I'll Find You.*"

"Fair enough. I'll try not to dim down the action too much or he'll be singing *Someday I lost you.*"

Ambrose did not think this was very funny.

The costumes were one of the unalloyed successes in this production. Sibyl re-appears at the Paris flat wearing the same travelling clothes from our first encounter with her. This made sense, but Alison objected and wanted a different costume. Doreen drew the line at that and so Alison capitulated, mainly because the evening dress she had for Act One was so gorgeous. She was ecstatic about it. If the blue sheath rehearsal dress had given her confidence, this slinky number, in pink, turned her into a young Greta Garbo as soon as she put it on. Amanda wore an extravagant pair of lounging pyjamas for the action in Paris and a similar fashionable evening gown for Act One. Ruth supplied her own negligee for the first entrance. Very daring, I thought, for a spinster schoolmarm.

Owen Ready's wife Janice was invariably in charge of makeup, even if she was in the cast. Her garish and colourful dress sense seemed to go with the ability she showed with the rouge and powder. If it was a large cast she seemed able to draft in someone from Boltons Beauty Salon in the town, whose promise was, 'We are hair to beautify you'. We were not a very sophisticated community. Such added resources also helped if there were wigs or hairstyles out of the ordinary, as was the case with *When We Are Married.* You will recall that in that play Janice had the part of Lottie, the loose woman, and she had great fun in making up her own face. She would not have been out of place on a corner in Soho or as a member of an Arabian harem. Ambrose persuaded her to tone it down; it might, he said, be suitable for a chorus girl in the the cowboy world of the Wild West but not quite the thing for the West Riding.

Although, as I have said, Jeremy Cowen was one of the few members to emerge unscathed from that production, that did not happen until he had made his amends to the colourful and extrovert Janice. Even though he was a new member he let it be known he was an experienced hand at this amateur dramatic lark, a thoroughly knowledgeable thespian. Not that he overplayed the situation but this assurance led him to criticise the dress that Janice was to wear in the play. Unfortunately he did not direct his views towards Ambrose, who would probably have told him that, 'Decisions on dress belonged to the Director, old boy, but he was listening to what was said and might suggest she should not wear that hat.' Instead, the foolish man made his remarks to Roger, and they were overheard.

I must tell you about the dressing rooms at the Village Hall. Well, to begin with, the use of the plural is misleading but firstly, to describe the auditorium itself. It is not the typical Village Hall, used for minor church activities or as a community centre. Yes, it is used for jumble sales and Scottish country dancing, but the facilities, in many respects, are rather better than normal. There is a spacious foyer with more than adequate cloakrooms, an alcove that contains a fixed bar with a refrigerator and a well equipped kitchen. The other valuable asset is a large store at the rear of the building, with a loading bay, where we store our scenery in some comfort and next to that is a walk-in closet where the stock of costumes is housed. And then, at the rear of the hall, are two glassed in areas, one for the lighting man and the other for the Director.

Those are all the plus factors that we are lucky to have. The not-so-good features are the stage, how we would have liked an extra ten feet of depth, and the chairs the paying public sit on; top-of-the-range plastic stackable. Inevitable; there could not be any permanent seating considering the multiplicity of uses.

And finally, behind the stage, is the dressing room. When we were not in occupation, this chamber is used for meetings of the Church Parish Council, Alcoholics Anonymous, Victim Support and similar bodies but when a theatre, it provides a very adequate dressing room with two long mirrors fixed to opposite walls. Each of these had a series of strip lights above; really quite professional, except – there is only one such room.

Who had designed it so, no one knew, but it had to be used by both the lady and gentleman artistes. There was much talk, at nearly every Committee Meeting, about forming a permanent division of the room but the Church Council adamantly refused any changes. Therefore, for many years, an old canvas backdrop was introduced, in some manner or other, to divide the sexes.

Back to *When We Are Married*. Before the Dress Rehearsal proper Ambrose had decided that for the penultimate run-through costumes, but not make-up, should be worn. It was at this time that Jeremy's words about Janice's costume drifted over the curtain. She is easy-going but no lady likes to have her sense of dress impugned, particularly by a man not her husband – and a newcomer at that. She muttered under her breath, added another vivid scarf to her ensemble, and began to plan her revenge.

At the Dress Rehearsal she was particularly careful with Jeremy's makeup. Ambrose loved these occasions. The General had brought his troops to the front line and is ready to deliver the few final rousing words that will lead them into victory.

"Everyone on stage please. Leave the curtains open. Sam. Lights full up please. Let the dog see the rabbit."

In dribs and drabs the cast move on to the stage.

"Come on ladies and gentlemen, boys and girls. One line only please. Now, before I begin the usual check Sam, when I give the word, spotlights on all. Owen, you do not need to show any signs of inebriation yet, or did you visit the Bull on the way here? Alison. Move closer to the middle, there's a sweet girl. Sam. Action."

The faces of the cast were suddenly bathed in a harsh yellow light.

"Good God, Jeremy. Do you feel ill? You look like a ghost. I think I can see straight through your head to the property lady standing behind you."

Everyone turned towards the luckless Herbert Soppitt. It was extraordinary. Until the full lights had been introduced no one had seen any flaws in his make-up, but now, he looked like Bella Lugosi or Dracula, or is it Boris Karloff. He would have done very well as the ghost of Banquo, or the one in Hamlet. His face was as pale as watered-down milk that contrasted with eyes where the mascara made them appear to be protruding beyond his cheeks as if on stalks. What an artist she was. You can accuse the female of the species of many faults but in matters of dress, leave well alone.

No harm was done. Cleansing cream quickly destroyed the masterpiece and Janice explained to Ambrose the background. We all thought it was a famously good joke, except for Jeremy, whose sense of humour did not seem to stretch that far.

One of the most important of the non-acting roles in Societies like ours is that of 'Publicity' – a catch-all word that covers the myriad duties involved in informing our fans that a new production is forthcoming. This entails dealing with the printing of posters, playbills, tickets and the programmes but the most difficult job for the unfortunate landed with this role is persuading local business people of the advantages of advertising in this programme. Not an easy task because there aren't any. Advantages, that is. No one buys anything extra after seeing an advertisement in a theatre programme – if anyone even looks at them. It is extortion. A plea to help keep culture alive in our town.

With publicity for *Private Lives* there was a surprising development at the emergency Committee meeting called to talk about pianos. Before Roger expressed his view on Alison, the Chairman intervened. I think he sensed that this was going to be one of our more successful efforts and therefore he would join the bandwagon and involve himself more than his wont. Not much more of course; he did not attend any of the rehearsals or offer to design the poster, but he did intercede in an attempt to disturb the sloth of our Honorary Treasurer.

It seemed that Trev had finally spotted that the money-man made little contribution to the activities of the society, even less than the Chairman himself. Perhaps he did not like losing his position as the premier 'do nothing' in the group – or, amazingly, was he finally recognizing my contribution. Had he discovered who prepares the Treasurer's Annual Statement and writes his speech?

"Jackson, I took careful note of what you said at the AGM. The more advertising we can sell the more funds we have for more ambitious productions. As you know, better than anyone, the set Vera had to hire for the Wizard cost an arm and a leg, as did the bonnets in the 'When we Marry' play. We therefore need to do better. I've already lined up the Crossley Manor Hotel for a page in the programme. You know we have our meetings there, and I think Moultons Brewery will also oblige. Chairman is in the Rotary. So, I've had a brainwave. I think you should offer to be in charge of Publicity and show us all how it's done."

Even George Thurston Brown sat up and took notice at this surprising development but as for Jackson, he became suddenly very pale.

"Mr Chairman. Quite right. Good for the coffers. The brewery. Splendid ale. Want to help, of course. Busy time at the Council. Problems with Council Tax. Re-grading exercise."

He even looked at me as though I was going to extricate him from this dangerous moment.

"Good. Delighted. Jackson. Just the man, but do not forget Singletons. Jasper was surprised not to be asked last time."

The Treasurer was busy loosening his tie as Trevor continued.

"Splendid. Ambrose. What other gaps are there? Dolores will be doing the makeup as usual, I presume."

"You mean Janice, yes, Chairman. And lucky to have Doreen in charge of costumes. We want to look at our best for this one."

And so to bed, as the saying goes. Whatever happens, the programme he is now in charge of will show that publicity has been assigned to Jackson Tollemache and he cannot wriggle out of that one. Of course, I could see what would happen as soon as he had recovered from the shock; he would be knocking at my door and I let him come knocking. In fact, I decided I would encourage him to turn to me and have some fun teasing him while he did so.

He came into the bank the next day to ask for change for a five pound note and, in passing, asked if I could pop round to his office when I was free; had some Society business to discuss. We finished cashing up early on Friday of that week so I hurried home to change my shirt before entering the Dragon's Den. By George, what a Dragon.

My near-diaphanous blouse was subject to close scrutiny before he asked me to sit down. As I did I moved the chair back, well away from the desk, so he could see that I had crossed my silken clad legs. I then uncrossed them. Not exactly Sharon Stone but I could see small beads of perspiration forming on his forehead. I could also read his thoughts. Were his half-hearted advances to be finally recognized?

"May. Publicity for the next one. Hope I can enlist you as my Lieutenant?"

"I'll do what I can but I'm busy with rehearsals, the AGM of the tennis club is just around the corner and I have two assignments for the Open University to finish before opening night."

"Good. Now, let's draw up a list of the people you might approach."

At this I leaned forward so he would be sure to catch the full impact of the Dior perfume I had applied before leaving home. I said nothing, but parted my lips and showed him the tip of my tongue protruding from between my delicate teeth.

"Perhaps we could meet one evening to discuss. There's that nice little pub at Lower Marston."

"Jackson. Didn't know you knew about the Green Man. Do you and your wife go there often?"

"No. Just heard about it. Mavis does not go out much."

"Do you?"

"Well no, neither do I, but I'm sure I can get away for an hour. On my way to cricket practice."

"But Jackson. You don't play cricket."

"I'm thinking of joining."

"Do you bat or bowl?"

By this time he was totally confused. Was he winning or losing? I put him out of his misery.

"All right. There's no rehearsal on Monday. Green Man. Seven o'clock."

As it happened I had visited this hostelry recently with Adrian Spencer, the young reporter from *The Record*. We met again after that first interview when he came into the bank to arrange the transfer of his account from a Birmingham branch. He seemed pleased to see me again and we have met, outside of working hours, on a couple of occasions since then. I tell you this because of my plan for the next Monday.

I claimed the ladies privilege of arriving late and as I walked into the Saloon Bar, in my highest heels, Jackson rose to his feet and as he leaned forward in an attempt to kiss me on the cheek knocked over the pint he had already purchased. He failed in the kissing operation but was slightly more efficient in securing a cloth from the barman to soak up the spilt ale.

"May. Sorry about that. You look charming."

"Thank you. Now, straight down to business. I said I would help and so I will. Here is a list of people you might approach about advertisements in the programme, this is the name of the man at Spire who deals with printing the tickets and the programmes and Ambrose says would you please consult with him before you decide on the design for the poster."

I had carefully rehearsed this little speech. Strange; there was no evidence of being tongue tied, nor any stage fright.

"Let me buy you a drink to replace that one."

"No. It will be my pleasure. What would you like?"

"Many thanks. I'll have a gin and tonic and Adrian always drinks Carlsberg. He'll be here in a minute, just parking the car."

The disconsolate figure of Jackson going to order drinks was the sign for Adrian to appear, as planned. On our way home he berated me. Told me I was a fiend and that it was a very cruel trick. Me, a fiend. I'll be stroking Adrian's hair next.

As you can see, even at this early stage, one consequence of our *Private Lives* seems to have been the radical effect it was having on the Players Honorary Secretary. My insignificance is still primary; an unrecognised cog in that great wheel of theatrical activity but to my amazement I seem to have become, on a minor scale, somewhat manipulative or perhaps to be more accurate, devious. Other than the Jackson jape, I can give you another instance. In this play music has an important role even if, to use the Master's words, it is cheap and potent, and Ambrose realised this fact from the beginning. As Vera was helping Roger with the voice coaching, he contemplated asking her to be in charge of sound effects but before he did, I made a suggestion.

"Ambrose. The music. You have said how vital this is. Coward and music go together like Lee and Perrins."

"Not sure the name of a sauce is appropriate for our dear Noël, but you are right. He has composed some of the greatest examples of popular music of the twentieth century."

"You have not yet met the new reporter at *The Record*, but I think he wants to join the Players and he tells me he has a large collection of music tapes."

"So what."

"Would you like me to ask him if he would do sound effects? The music has to be just right."

"I believe Brenda was thinking of asking Vera, but by all means ask the young man. What's his name? Is he reliable?"

I know he played tapes in his car, until I asked him to turn them off, but I doubted if he could be labelled as a musicologist. On the other hand, it seemed to me that not too much expertise was needed to turn a knob or press a button on some machine or other; and I had already calculated that it would be quite pleasant to have him around at some of the rehearsals. Without any hesitation he refused to occupy this role. Quite adamant – but eventually he was persuaded.

I helped him and pointed out where music of some sort or other was required. Even before any of the characters appear on stage we are told that, 'There is an orchestra playing not very far off.' We hear it again when Amanda lets Elyot know that she is on the next balcony by joining in the song the orchestra is playing, a different melody, and he is humming. This is referred to as, 'a sentimental romantic little tune'. A little later:

ELYOT:That orchestra has a remarkably small repertoire.
AMANDA:They don't seem to know anything but this, do they?
[She sits on the balustrade, and sings it, softly. Her eyes are
looking out to sea, and her mind is far away. ELYOT watches her
while she sings. When she turns to him at the end, there are tears in
her eyes. He looks away awkwardly and lights another cigarette.]
ELYOT:You always had a sweet voice, Amanda.

It seemed to me that all of this was a fairly routine affair for an experienced, or even an inexperienced, sound effects operative. Two different pieces of music: press the right button at the right time but in Act Two when Elyot sits at the piano, joined soon after by Amanda, and: 'They sing several old refrains from dead and gone musical comedies finishing with the song that brought them together again in the first act.', rather more expertise is required. I went to Vera. I told her a little about Adrian and she dealt with making a recording of piano music that Roger and Ruth could pretend to play as they sang. Neither had the piano playing skills required to execute this for real but the singing needed to be genuine. Vera told me Roger was making good progress. Fortunately, Ruth had a very clear singing voice; she sounded exactly as Mr Coward would have wanted. I left it to Vera to choose the music from the 'dead and gone musical comedies'. She may well have been in some of them.

It was Brenda who suggested the sound effects for Act One. One of the first lines in the play refers to the lights of a yacht reflected in the water and so it was not difficult to envisage how to advance this image by providing a background of the noise made by the tide gently lapping a shallow beach with the addition of an occasional seagull squawk. If the thought was obvious, and simple, the provision thereof was rather more difficult. Eric offered to take a microphone into Waxen Woods and record whatever birdsong was available and as for the tide, he suggested a kitchen sink filled with old newspapers where the tap is turned on and off at regular intervals. Neither Ambrose nor Brenda was very impressed. I wondered if there was somewhere, a library of sound effects and I believe this is how the problem was solved. I never enquired because at that time I was finding it necessary to spend too many evenings with Adrian discussing popular music from before his time and the intricacies of the tape recorder.

However, he did become involved in those seaside noises. They were installed on a separate machine that was placed next to the music one and all he was required to do was to start it off at the beginning of Act One and extinguish the sounds as Elyot and Amanda exit those convenient balconies. He managed that very successfully until the second night of the production when, so he alleges, the sleeve of his jacket made contact with the volume control so that the first half dozen lines between Sibyl and Elyot were submerged under what sounded like a force ten gale accompanied by an excerpt from Hitchcock's, *The Birds*. The audience, when they realised what had happened, roared with laughter but I believe if Adrian had been more our Director's size there could well have been some serious physical damage inflicted during the interval on that clumsy newspaperman. He pleaded *mea culpa* but I think it was another example of a mischievous nature, which I suppose I was beginning to find mildly attractive.

Chapter Six

The Rehearsals

BLOCKING OUT the moves for the play was not too difficult. Coward was both actor and playwright and he therefore knew how important these were so the script is precise as to who should be where at any given moment. The tooing and frowing on the terraces needs to be crisp and efficient; it is part of the charm of the play that we see, seamlessly, the two couples, firstly as newlyweds, then the formerly wed and then the discarded pair. The first exit of Sibyl and Elyot was never going to be a problem. If Alison was unsure, which early on she often was, Roger would take her firmly by the elbow and if necessary lift her off her feet and leave, Stage Left. Victor then appears and Jeremy always delayed his entrance sufficiently for the audience to catch their breath after the quick-fire repartee of the departed pair and to begin to foresee what happens next. The timing is even more important when Elyot alone looks at the moon. The playgoer either knows, or can guess, what happens next and Amanda appearing on the adjoining terrace needs to be anticipated.

"Count to ten Ruth, and then appear with the cocktails."

Ambrose, very sensibly, had Ruth practice with a tray from an early point during rehearsals. The image of a sophisticated lady is rather spoilt if the champagne glasses slide off the tray and crash to the floor before Elyot and Amanda have a chance to meet. Scenes that involve eating and drinking are always capable of being turned into disaster sites and we have had some powerful examples of this. In *Separate Tables,* hot-pot or goulash or whatever it was, spilt everywhere and the Wilde play was not much better. George Robertson might not be much of a success as an auctioneer, or as an actor, but he is a champion muncher of muffins. No wonder that when he played Algy he was inaudible most of the time; his mouth was clogged up with those confections. Ambrose ordered the imitation muffins to be made less palatable but George still stuffed himself with the rounds of three-day-old bread provided. They only made him gag even more and become irritatingly incoherent.

Ambrose was devoting all of his skill and energy into justifying his choice of Alison to play Sibyl when all of a sudden he had another problem on his hands. Roger. He began to forget his lines. It was as if London Bridge had finally fallen down.

"Roger. You've missed out two lines. Are you unwell?"

"Sorry. Can't think what came over me. Temporary aberration. Had a bad night, I think. Better leave early if you don't mind."

On that occasion Ambrose was concentrating on Act Two so without his Elyot it looked as though it was going to be a wasted rehearsal until Jeremy spoke up. He and Alison were present because it was hoped to do the opening scene of Act Three as well which was of course the platform for my performance.

"I know most of Elyot's part. Shall I stand-in so at least Ruth gets some practice?"

At this our Amanda looked dubious but as Ambrose accepted Jeremy's offer she fell in line even though I knew she wanted to have as little to do with him as possible. When she compliments Elyot on his 'little dressing gown' and has the line:

Do you mind if I come round and kiss you

Both Jeremy and she increased the space between themselves and went straight on to the next line.

But the tension between these two was not at the forefront of my mind. What was the matter with our paragon? Had this anything to do with property development? My ruminations came to an end as Ambrose reached Act Three. It was finally becoming clear to him that Ruth was not very friendly towards Jeremy, and he rather hurried through Act Two, coming to my big moment earlier than I had expected.

Ruth had helped me with the French pronunciation and I felt confident in that department but, even though the audience was now limited to the Director, Ruth, Jeremy and Alison, I still became tongue tied. I managed the first line.

Bon jour, Madame.

and nearly got my next line right, but when Sibyl asked me what time it was, I seized up completely. It was inevitable. Ambrose might have a difficulty with Roger to cope with, in addition to his Sibyl, and so he could not be bothered with a dithering Louise.

"May. I know you have this problem, but I like having you around. You brew an excellent pot of tea, and if I recall you had some hand in solving the piano predicament. Stay on as the maid, but be a silent one. At the opening of Act Three you walk on with the shopping – a string of garlic around your neck, and two baguettes under each arm – look amazed at what you see and then disappear into the kitchen; but don't forget to draw the curtains and bring the coffee on near the end. I'm sure Noël won't mind. You make enough noise as you come in, and go out, so that Victor and Sibyl awake and we can then begin the scene with that young lady saying, 'What are we to do?'"

I was relieved. I would still get my name in the programme and provided I did not drop the bread, or fall over, it was risk-free – and as far as the overall play was concerned, Louise's contribution had no import. No one disagreed with Ambrose's decision. Except for Alison, all were more concerned with the unknown plight of Roger than the demotion of Louise to a non-speaking role.

As foreseen, I did get my name in the programme, but not as Louise. Two weeks before opening night, Tricia made a direct approach to Ambrose, by-passing me, to tell him she had split up with her objectionable boyfriend, was getting bored with the empty evenings and could she please have her part as the maid returned to her. She must have charmed him, she can be quite attractive when she tries, because he agreed. He knew she would manage the few lines involved, but to be fair to him he did not simply discard me.

"May, Tricia came to see me today. At the shop. Wants to do the maid. I explained about you but then saw this as a blessing in disguise. I think that after me you understand and love this play more than anyone else in the Society and I know you will be more valuable as the prompt than as a silent Louise. Particularly for Alison's sake. She's doing well but I would feel easier if I knew you were there to give her the line if she has a lapse of memory."

"But what about Joan? She's scheduled to be the prompt."

"Yes. But she is also involved with props and I know she will be delighted to only have the one job."

"All right then. I think that's for the best."

Little did I know how important this change was to be?

In my view, the prompt is often the unsung hero of the amateur stage. If everything goes according to plan and all the actors know their lines, or even if they do not but are sufficiently skilled to avoid silences and gaps in the action that the audience can perceive, it is a very boring task. Being available to whisper forgotten words while sitting out of sight, but hopefully within earshot, and concentrating on every line – and then never being called into action, not once, is not much fun. Indeed, the same lines might become imbued with such a familiarity that they can send the poor unfortunate holder of this post into a catatonic state of nervous hysteria. As the curtains fall they rise from their lonely position like a zombie, only able to rejoin the human race after a large glass of some spirituous sustenance. Even so, the occupant of the prompt's chair at the corner of the stage is an essential member of the ensemble.

On the professional stage they may have a less important role than with us because experienced actors can extemporise when a lapse occurs without needing any outside assistance. I do not know if that is the case, but there are all sorts of stories about how actors bypass the prompt. Adrian says there are lots of funny tales about happenings in the cricket world but I can hardly believe they measure up to those that emanate from the stage.

AE Matthews, who was over ninety when he died, said that during his last years on the stage he never left for the theatre until he had read *The Times* obituary column to see if he was still alive. Well, there is a famous prompt story concerning him. When during a play he answered the telephone and then forgot his lines he quickly found a solution; he handed the instrument over to a young and

inexperienced actor he was playing against and said, 'It's for you.'
I do not think even Roger Scotland would be that cruel. Another
story about an actor in a Repertory Company who, lost for words
desperately whispers to the prompt: 'What's the line?' only to be
greeted by the reply: 'What's the play?' Our worst experience was
when Monica had the job, for one night only. In answer to the
whispered: 'What's the line' she replied: 'What page are we on.'

Further information about Roger came from an unusual source.
Surprisingly, my mother decided she and I should attend morning
service at St George's on the Sunday closest to the twentieth
anniversary of my father's demise. This had never happened before.
Perhaps she was feeling her age? She did not curtail her Saturday
night frolic at the Bull but woke me early the next day and off we
went. It felt like something out of Dickens. My mother has a guilty
secret and after all these years she needs to find salvation, confess
and atone for her sin! We both dressed the part, well at least my
Mam wore a hat and I had a dark blue skirt and black stockings.

The Rev Bob was delighted to see us; made quite a fuss as we left
the church. Rather ignored the regulars. When he told me his wife
and the children had gone to visit an aged aunt, and he was going
back to the rectory to open a tin of beans, I asked him to come and
have roast beef and Yorkshire pudding with us. Mam and I had not
discussed the menu for our Sunday repast. Thanks to Eric, it was
always the same; the best cut of beef, either sirloin or silverside, or
some superior leg of lamb or pork. The cleric jumped at the chance. I
expect his normal Sunday meal, cooked by Hortense, was a thin beef
stew or even a cottage pie. Or, now I come to think of it, is she not
a vegetarian? No wonder he looks so pale and thin, and no wonder
he agreed to a second helping. It really was out of Trollope. Insisted
he should carve the joint. Who did he think did the honours when
there were just two ladies at the table: the ghost of my father, spilling
tobacco ash over the nicely larded side of cow?

There was a reward however for this kindly act. Bob had drunk
three glasses of Rioja with his beef and was persuaded to partake in
a glass of port to go with Mam's rhubarb crumble. Afterwards he
opted for a cup of tea rather than coffee. This pleased the head cook
greatly. 'Can't be doing with that coffee' was her usual response but,

whatever, he was in a relaxed mood as he sipped his Tetley's. He did not stutter once.

"How is the play going, May?"

"As usual. Same alarums and excursions."

"How is Roger coping?"

"His normal confident self."

"Oh. I thought the problem with Brenda might have put him off."

"Problem?"

I tried to say this as though hinting I knew very well to what he was referring.

"Not that she has consulted me, but it seems extraordinary that it should have happened in that ménage."

I said nothing and offered him another small glass of port.

"Evidently a casual acquaintance. Perhaps you cannot blame her, if it is true that he has got them into financial difficulties. It does seem to have increased his aggression."

What on earth was he talking about? Roger spent all their money and when his wife complains he blacks her eye? Nonsense. Not in the household of our prima donnas.

"I am a little concerned about the children."

Good heavens, I thought, it sounds serious. Or is the Rev Bob in the middle of a drunken ramble: something he had read in the *News of the World?*

In her capacity as Stage Manager I had seen more of Brenda than normal, particularly when it came to introducing Adrian as the potential sound effects member of her team. As he was not quite sure what this was all about we had a special meeting with her, that involved me, to discuss what the other ditties might be besides *Someday I'll Find You.* She seemed somewhat dubious as to Adrian's ability in this department but after he had gone back to the offices of *The Record,* some deadline or other, I thought this would be an ideal moment to ask about Roger's early exit from the last rehearsal.

People do seem to confide in me: perhaps it is my own reserve that is responsible but you will not be surprised that I funked the issue and we parted hoping Adrian would be able to rise to the occasion. Nevertheless, my reluctance to raise this with Brenda did not prevent me from speculating what her reply might have been.

"Yes, he was home early. My fault entirely I'm afraid. I've talked to Ruth about this but it is not general knowledge. She's rather an innocent, don't you think, while I believe for all your withdrawn nature, your apparently bland personality, you are really quite what they call 'a woman of the world'."

By a shake of the head I indicate that this was far from the case.

"You probably know the script of that Coward thing pretty much by now. In many ways, glad I'm not playing Amanda. Don't you cringe at the line about women should be struck regularly like gongs?"

"Yes. Very much so. He wrote the part for Gertrude Lawrence, and really Amanda is the best role in the play, but there are times when the misogyny grates, like the gong thing, however light-hearted it is supposed to be."

"Precisely, and you will recall the bit about men can have affairs, but not women."

"Yes, and her reply, if I've got it right. 'It doesn't suit men for women to be promiscuous'."

"How true to life: or is it? I won't mention the affair Roger had during *Separate Tables* but I did tell you he was thinking about getting into property development if, and when, he retires. Well, without going into detail, he began to dabble earlier than any move to retire and, most unusually, he kept it to himself. You know May, he can be a bit high-handed at times, but we get on well together. Like attracts like, perhaps. I've got him in my system, and he's been a relatively good husband and father."

I try to look as though I agree with her.

"So what caused him to start keeping secrets, I cannot imagine. When I found out I was really angry but I became even angrier when I discovered that he might be in for losing a fair proportion of our savings. All these years when I might have been a mega-star of stage and screen I have been looking after the house and children while he charges extortionally high fees for his legal expertise. So I consider those savings are half mine. It was our very first serious quarrel."

"I think you know, Brenda, he does not seem to like me and frankly, I'm not very fond of him. He is always so superior."

"That's true. He cannot help it. He has worked hard to get to where he is. Came from a poor family, you know. Father was a railway porter and mother a bit wayward. He wasn't like this when we met in Bristol, but the struggle he has had since seems to have clad him with a hard protective shell that is difficult to pierce. Anyway, I refused to go away on holiday with him. We were taking the children to Weston-Super-Mare: I left them with him and went off on a jaunt on my own, in high dudgeon."

"I thought I saw him buying ice cream in the High Street one day."

"I was so mad it must have sent me mad. I drove off. Thought I would go to see my sister who lives near Edinburgh but I never got there. Stopped at some smart country hotel. Met a young man in the bar and allowed myself to be flattered by his attention sufficiently to spend the night with him – and I enjoyed it, let me tell you. Very odd. When Roger is in a play he seems to concentrate all his energies into that at the expense of any activity in the bedroom. It does not matter what the part is. Casanova, fop or a virginal Hamlet; I suppose it's a case of 'all passion spent'. Nevertheless, I was ashamed at my conduct so before the young man awoke, his name was Rufus, I was in my car heading back to Roger."

My mouth drops open.

"Reached home before the children were up – half term – and with tears streaming down my cheeks told him what had happened. He was like ice. I thought he was going to hit me and so my anger over the property business returned. I might even have used the Coward line about promiscuity. And that night he went to the rehearsal, the one he left early. On his return I apologised again, both for my actions and invoking the great Noel, and he then said he was sorry about the property secret. It was a fulfilling reconciliation. I think you'll find he will be back to his normal self the next time you see him as Elyot."

What an imagination I have. No doubt the truth is Roger had just eaten a bad oyster at lunchtime and was suffering from a pernicious form of food poisoning that affects some of the lobes of the brain.

On the other hand, what was the Rev Bob alluding to?

At the next rehearsal, Roger was back to his usual loathsome self and made no reference to his earlier lapse. Ambrose hardly seemed to notice. There was a real spring in our Director's step, mainly because Alison was making such progress. Perhaps he had made the right choice after all although I was still concerned that the age gap, particularly between her and the two men, put the balance of the piece at risk. He, of course, had no intention of advancing Alison's age; no instructions to Janice to insert some lines around the eyes or darken the makeup. Doreen's contribution followed suit. When she proudly displayed Sibyl's evening gown it was clearly meant for a girl in her early twenties and that only reinforced my view that some of our audience might see Elyot as a cradle snatcher. Costumes for the men helped to camouflage the fact that they were both nearer fifty than forty but this did not, for a moment, dim the spark that Ambrose was coaxing out of his Sibyl.

The differential with Ruth was not such a problem and she told me that Alison's obvious youth was inspiring our Amanda to be more loose and energetic, more athletic and lively than the middle aged opponents. We talked about this.

"Ruth. May I ask you a question?"

"Of course."

"How do you feel about Roger? I think he is a mean-mannered brute but am I just prejudiced because he tends to treat me like one of his office juniors?"

"Brute is rather strong, isn't it, but he's not very warm I admit. I sometimes feel sorry for Brenda but I'm sure she holds up her end all right, and they seem devoted to each other."

"I did hear there had been a small contretemps."

"So did I, but it's not our business is it."

I felt as though I had been rather put in my place. Must ask Bob to lunch again.

"Of course. Not very warm is your description."

"Yes, even unlikable, but he is a very good actor and has already got Elyot's light touch perfectly, particularly in Act Two. The stiffness disappears as if he is shedding an overcoat."

"Reluctantly, I must admit you are right."

"It's a real challenge for me. Because away from the stage he is mostly unfriendly I am determined to show an Amanda that is more than Elyot's equal and the fact that in real life he is more than fifteen years older than me should be reflected on the stage. He doesn't get much exercise, you know, and even though I do say it myself, I am very fit. Chasing those young girls around the hockey pitch is a great help. It's going to stand me in good stead. During the fight scene I'll have him puffing and blowing by the end of the Act."

"What will Ambrose say to that?"

"Will he notice? I think he is satisfied that Jeremy and Roger and me are so experienced he can leave us to develop our parts by ourselves while he concentrates on Alison."

"Yes. I agree. They are so in love."

"May. Don't talk such nonsense."

There was another factor in the playing between Ruth and Roger other than the fight scenes that, as the rehearsals progressed, had an unforeseen but interesting result. It would seem that because of the measure of antagonism there was between them off-stage, this exaggerated, as if by magic, the sexual tension that Coward wanted to be represented in the relationship between Elyot and Amanda. As a result this was, in our production, ratcheted up to such an extent that in Act Two you could well have thought we were witnessing a sophisticated Mellors and an aggressive Lady Chatterley in a version by Tennessee Williams.

Once again I exaggerate but there is no doubt that Roger would not have been as sexually aggressive an Elyot if he had been making love to an Amanda who was also his wife and naturally, as it seemed to me, Ruth became more ardent to compensate for any thought that she might be regarded as an interloper. Ambrose allowed this to flourish: he probably thought he had engineered the rejection of Brenda to achieve this result. Fanciful of course, but he was clever enough to accept the consequences of his actions and revel in them.

This situation added another dimension to the scenes where Amanda and Elyot move from intense passion to the bickering.

ELYOT: *Angel. Angel. Angel.*
[He kisses her passionately.

AMANDA [struggling slightly]: No, Elyot, stop now, stop –
ELYOT: Why should I stop? You know you adore being made love
to.
AMANDA [through his kisses]: It's so soon after dinner.

This last line always produced a laugh but because of the electricity between the protagonists, Roger's delivery of Elyot's angry reaction was one of real frustration rather than humour.

By the time Ruth was fully in her stride, she rather shocked Ambrose, and Roger I think, when during one rehearsal she began to shrug off her pyjama top during the most intense act of passion which is interrupted by the telephone.

[He catches at her hand and kisses it, and then her arm, until
he is standing up, embracing her ardently. She struggles a little,
half laughing, and breaks away, but he catches her, and they finish
up on the sofa again, clasped in each other's arms, both completely
given up to the passion of the moment, until the telephone bell rings
violently, and they both spring apart.]

I thought she was marvellous during that particular sofa sequence, but she did not go quite so far thereafter.

As Alison improved Ambrose beamed like the Eddystone lighthouse. She would not have noticed, but there are some lines in Act Three that have echoes of the tea party between Gwendoline and Cicely in the Wilde play. I am sure Ambrose heard what I did and encouraged his protégé to lapse into a lisp at this point.

AMANDA [sociably]:What would one do without one's morning coffee?
That's what I often ask myself.
ELYOT:Is it?
AMANDA [withering him with a look]: Victor, sugar for Sibyl.
[To SIBYL] It should be absurd for me to call you anything but Sibyl,
wouldn't it?
SIBYL [not to be outdone]: Of course; I shall call you Mandy.
[Amanda represses a shudder.]

Minor cracks in the steady progress of the rehearsals began to appear during the fight scenes, as Ruth had predicted. If the mismatching of opponents in the Elyot versus Amanda contest were exaggerated because of Ruth's machinations, the difference in the abilities of the other two were shown up even more starkly by the sprightliness of Alison, without any design whatsoever. Even Ambrose began to see this.

The last line of the play is Sibyl's.

Stop it! Stop it! You insufferable great brute!

The stage instructions then read:

She slaps his face hard, and he takes her by the shoulders and shakes her like a rat, as AMANDA and ELYOT go smilingly out of the door, with their suitcases, and –

Alison loved it. She told me it was the best bit in the whole of this boring play. Ambrose encouraged her to slap hard, and she did. On the first occasion Victor reeled and Alison was ten feet away across the stage before he could contemplate any shaking. Ruth could see what was happening so before Jeremy could pursue his quarry across the stage, she smiled at Elyot and was out of the door like greased lightning, cue for the curtain to fall, with Victor still stranded. The next time they tried, Jeremy was ready and just managed to catch the sleeve of Alison's dress before she skipped away, but he was not always even that successful.

Ruth's contribution during the other fight scene was equally intriguing. Firstly, here are the full set of stage instructions.

At this point in the proceedings they trip over a piece of carpet, and fall on to the floor, rolling over and over in paroxysms of rage. VICTOR and SIBYL enter quietly, through the open door, and stand staring at them in horror. Finally AMANDA breaks free and half gets up, ELYOT grabs her leg, and she falls against a table, knocking it completely over.

She rushes back at ELYOT who is just rising to his feet, and gives him a stinging blow, which knocks him over again. She rushes blindly off Left, and slams the door…

Ruth executed the rolling over and over with such vigour Roger had no alternative but to follow suit. This so incapacitated him that invariably he failed to grab Amanda's leg as she got up, which gave her the opportunity to knock over the table dangerously close to her opponent. She then screams out the last line of the Act. Thank goodness that honour was not accorded to the out-of-breath Roger, and then, taking a leaf out of Alison's book, Ruth pushes out whatever breath is left in his lungs by the savagery of her final assault.

When I reached home that night I looked at our insurance policy to see what cover we had for bones broken during the rehearsal process. Ambrose followed a different tack. He could see the potential in the fight scenes to add a further aspect of dynamic activity to the otherwise wordy exchanges between the two couples. He raised this at the next rehearsal and informed us that he had recruited Owen Ready as a 'fight adviser' and he was expected at any moment to begin his instruction. What a brainwave. It was always fun to have Owen around and I recalled my mother telling me that he had been a useful amateur pugilist in his younger days. Appeared at the Albert Hall, so Mam said.

Owen was already on the premises when we were treated to some additional drama, the words and actions of which had no connection whatsoever with Mr Coward. In point of fact, there were not many words anyway. George arrived during Act One and, without permission from Ambrose, marched on to the stage just as Victor was saying to Amanda:

I'm glad I'm so normal.

Extraordinarily, the slow witted George picked up this line and told Jeremy that he was far from normal and that in fact he was a blackguard. He then punched him on the nose, turned on his heels and exited Stage Left before I could proffer to Victor my handkerchief to stem the flow of blood. George then left the hall. Ruth was on the verge of tears, I was inwardly applauding what had happened, particularly as my offer of first aid had initially not been recognized by the wounded man, and Ambrose was about to begin a series of little jumps.

The punch had been well directed, but not too powerful, and the blood soon stopped falling over Jeremy's upper lip whereupon he threw my handkerchief to the back of the stage. He was very pale. Not, I thought, from loss of blood, but because of that potent mixture of shame and anger, probably more of the former than otherwise. Ambrose came on stage to inspect the proboscis.

"I have never seen George so animated. Are you all right?"

"Yes. He's mad."

"What about?"

"Nothing. Unprovoked attack. Roger, can I sue him for damages?"

Our legal eagle seemed to view this event as mildly amusing.

"Police matter. Don't think you would get very far in the civil courts. Not too much damage. If every punch on the nose finished up in court we lawyers would be laughing all the way to the bank. Wonder what aroused him like that? Do you think the next step will be pistols at dawn?"

Jeremy ignored this and suggested to Ambrose that we get on with the rehearsal. Ruth never said a word but Owen whispered to me that he could not have done better himself. Evidently he approved of the way George had shaped up before delivering the classic left jab.

I was as a surprised as everyone else to see the mild-mannered George acting in this fashion, but it was very possible that except for he and me, no other member of the Society knew that I was the agent provocateur in this matter. Presumably Ruth and Jeremy could guess at the probable reason for George's offensive but I suspect that neither wanted this to be revealed, or talked about – certainly not between themselves. When I told George of the treatment Ruth had received at the hands of Jeremy I was betraying her trust and involving myself in something that was really no business of mine, which makes me look back to see what motive I had for involving her brother. I am sorry I did. I feel some shame – it was not my responsibility to be a champion for Ruth; it was the last thing she would have wanted and I therefore decided that when the play was over, I would confess my sins to her and apologise for being so foolish.

And that that was that. Other than the minor damage to the nose, and perhaps the more serious impact on his *armour propre*, Jeremy was not seriously injured and was clearly intent on ignoring what had happened. As for Ruth, she said nothing at the scene of the blow, nor afterwards – at least not until I told her what I had done when she said plenty – but eventually she forgave me and made fun of the whole affair, labelling me as an interfering old gossip.

Adrian was proving to be something of a washout in the music department, but I did discover an arena where he was more than proficient, namely the cricket field. I like the game but with other male friends in the past I have always expressed indifference without telling them that this stemmed from the fact that ladies are not allowed to be members of the MCC. Anyway, now there has been some relaxation in the rules on that subject, and because Adrian may have been more persuasive than the other flannelled fools I have known, I went to see him play.

He was already in the Town's first eleven and as I knew that some of the girls at Ruth's school now played the game, I asked if she would like to come with me. Adrian was the wicketkeeper. To my inexperienced eye he kept very tidily – you can see I have listened to Test Match Special on the BBC – but when going in to bat at number four, he was bowled first ball – by Jeremy.

Ruth and I were astonished to see him playing for a club side that toured the Midlands. I think they were called 'The Infidels', or something like that. We did not know he was interested in the game but besides dismissing our wicketkeeper cheaply, he bagged three more wickets and made thirty or so when batting at number six. Adrian found us a cup of tea during the interval between innings and Jeremy joined us. No doubt he was as surprised to see us as we were him. Ambrose is not a fan. I am not saying the subject was banned at rehearsals but, true to form, very few other subjects are ever discussed other than the current play or, just occasionally, a reference will be made to a previous production if pertinent to what we are currently engaged with.

Away from the Village Hall, Jeremy began to exhibit a gracious charm, even towards me, far removed from that of a male chauvinist assaulter of women and I began to see what had attracted Ruth initially. She was hesitant at first, but by the time 'The Infidels' went out to bat, she was more relaxed than I had seen her for some time. On reflection, I think they were actually named, 'The Incomparables'.

One of the most appealing aspects of Ambrose's character is the optimism. It is in my nature also: the jug is always half full in my eyes and not half empty. This trait could however be dangerous and you would have thought that past experience might have led to some planning against emergencies, even though when things had gone wrong in the past he had sometimes been lucky.

For instance, when Vera was playing Lady Bracknell. By the last night her laryngitis had rendered her totally speechless and there was no one to take over at such short notice. As a result we had a hilarious final performance with Owen Ready stepping in as an aristocratic pantomime dame after handing over his clerical garb, he was playing Canon Chasuble, to Ambrose. Doreen let out the dress to fit Owen's portly frame but the hats needed no adjustments, even if they could not be fastened to his sparse growth of hair with pins so those two marvellous items of headgear were taped to his shiny pate. The shoes might have been a problem but it was the work of a moment to lengthen the dresses to hide his plimsolls. Being the accomplished performer that he his, he managed to keep his shoes well hidden even when sitting down. He produced about fifty per cent of the lines, and adlibbed wildly, but it did not seem to matter.

Everyone enjoyed his performance and many in the audience thought it was the best portrayal of the august lady they had ever seen. The more serious problem was Tricia. She was playing the strait-laced Miss Prism but in the last act she developed an extreme attack of the giggles at the sight of Owen and as a result we were in danger of turning the dramatic finale into a farce. Fortunately, when she exits to fetch the handbag, Ambrose was able to bring her to her senses and he then accepted the adulation as though he had planned a substitute for Vera from day one. He had not: and neither did he have any emergency plan should anything befall anyone in the cast of *Private Lives*.

Of course, it was not always the actors that needed cover. Eric was scheduled as the Stage Manager for *When We Are Married* – and then what happened; he breaks his ankle. He is a wonderful extrovert fellow, our local butcher, but even so I was still amazed when Mam came home from work one day to say that Eric had bought a leather jacket and a pair of leather trousers and that before the week was over he intended to buy a motorcycle. Mid-life crisis, my mother said, but he went through with the scheme and on his second excursion, fell off the machine and broke his right ankle. He managed to continue his shop-keeping duties, perched on a stool, but had to withdraw as Stage Manager for the Priestley play. His replacement, Charlie Sacks, was a disaster. On two separate nights, the door to the hall of Helliwell house stuck fast and improbably everyone had to appear on stage through the conservatory.

This simply added to the many disasters of that particular production, but I recount this incident to emphasise that in amateur dramatics, if there is a chance of something going wrong, it will do so.

With *Private Lives* I considered the possibilities. On the technical side, the presence of Brenda as Stage Manager foretold calm waters but on the acting front, particularly with such a small cast, there was little back-up. Even if there was only one absentee, particularly on the male side, we were into serious trouble. I suppose it was just possible that Brenda could step in for either Sibyl or Amanda; more admirably for the latter as she would really be too old for the current Mrs Chase, and certainly so in comparison with Ruth. When I told Ambrose of my thoughts, and possible fears, he patted me on the cheek and told me not to worry my pretty little head about such things. He is enjoying this play, enormously – and I am beginning to like being told that I have a pretty head.

Perhaps to date my picture of the Society has been presented to you more in the strident form of a painting by Jackson Pollack but there are times when a family portrait by Gainsborough or the quiescent atmosphere of a Degas dance studio is more appropriate; we are not always in the grip of a crisis. Two weeks before opening night things seemed to be going swimmingly but I was still a little concerned that something really serious might be amiss with Roger.

Ambrose was a mite mercurial but had he really rejected Brenda because she had rejected him? And was Roger so in love with his wife that her absence from the stage had affected his own performance? I thought not. I believed Brenda when she said it was a good thing for the Players that they be split up for once but what a pity this had to occur at the time of a play made for their joint talents. It is possible that Ambrose invented the East Anglia farrago to ease Roger on to the sidelines; but why; there had to be a more serious reason? There is surely a more complex plot festering away underneath – and I assumed the lead actor in this had to be Ambrose. Is he more complicated than he appears to be?

Firstly, the Lothario thing. He ran Pottingers but I suspect the majority of the ownership is still in the hands of Iris. She had been brought up in the family business and I can see her as a four-year-old in the shop on Saturday mornings looking at the pretty pictures in the travel catalogues. As a teenager she is making the tea and dressing the windows for her grandfather and then keeping the books and explaining to her new husband that New Caledonia and New Zealand are different places, well away from Scotland. She had been a good teacher. Although I make fun of him he now runs the place very well and his cheerful and bubbly nature attract nearly all of his fellow citizens to look no further when holiday times came around. He did flirt with the lady travellers and with the young assistants but no one objected, least of all Iris. She thought it attracted more customers and was totally convinced of his fidelity.

She and Helen were close friends; they had been at school together and I would often see Brenda in their company. Helen even involved her in the Women's Institute. And so, what had happened to ruffle Ambrose's feathers and disrupt this relationship?

One night, after all had gone, Ambrose and I left the hall at the end of what had been the best rehearsal so far, even if Roger and Ambrose seemed even more distant. Alison was now in charge of the high heels and there had been a little more warmth between Amanda and Victor. Was this all due to the game of cricket? Ambrose was radiant. He was bubbly. He was over the moon. He was excited.

My hyperbole again, but he was rather pleased with himself. As I withdrew the heavy key from the exit door he kissed me on the back of my head, put his arms around me and gently attempted to fondle my breasts. The slap I administered to his cheek was in the same league as the one Ruth was administering nearly nightly to

Elyot; it was certainly enough to move Ambrose from the vertical. I helped him to his feet as we said sorry at the same time, but I could still see a twinkle in his eyes. I think he enjoyed it, despite the consequences.

"My dear girl. What came over me. Exultation. We are getting there. Best rehearsal yet. Sorry."

"I agree. Never mind."

"Why don't we celebrate? Let's tell Iris. Come home and have some coffee – or are you a girl who likes a dram of single malt?"

I am, and had two glasses at least, as did my host: Iris kept to the coffee. Alcohol generally lessens tensions. It did that night, beginning with me as I was emboldened to ask a question.

"Iris, I can confirm what Ambrose has said. Bit sticky to begin with, but except for the abject failure of Louise, by the way, Tricia is back, your dear husband has assembled a splendid cast."

"Do you miss Brenda?"

"I suppose so but Ruth is doing very well. It would be so interesting to eavesdrop at school to see if she retains any of Amanda when she says, 'Good morning, gells'. Do you know Ambrose if there is a theatrical version of Jean Brodie?"

"Yes, my dear, I believe there is. Maggie Smith if I recall correctly."

"But back to Brenda. She was of course the obvious choice. Why, Iris, do you think it didn't happen?"

They looked at each other. By a movement of the eyebrows Iris seemed to pass over to her husband some form of assent and as a result he began to answer my question

"May. You are a trustworthy and careful girl and a loyal member of the Players. For your ears only, as they say in the Bond films. The Scotlands, or more correctly Roger, is involved in a matter contrary to Pottingers' interests. Even worse, he did not have the decency to talk to Iris or me beforehand."

"Something to do with property?"

"How did you know that?"

"I heard a remark about Holmfield Farm."

"No. Nothing to do with that. Jackson said something along those lines and so, in the circumstances, I made a careful enquiry but there is nothing shady about that proposal. What concerns us is on a much larger scale. Have you heard about proposals for a supermarket in the town?"

"No. Can't say I have."

"Well, one of the big chains has been making enquiries about sites on the outskirts of the town, with no success. They then turned their attention to something smaller, but central. As you probably know, Turners furniture store next to us is not doing very well. Since the old man died it's rather gone downhill. Everybody goes to Ikea these days. Leslie wants to close down. Behind the shop is a large warehouse that stretches behind us as well."

"Yes. Not much used is it. The alley between the two buildings is, I believe, a regular Lovers Lane."

"Another good reason for its preservation. A year ago we were approached by a London agent to see if we would sell. I told them there were a number of young Pottinger/Percys coming along to take over the business and therefore, not for sale."

"Is there any danger of compulsory purchase?"

"You are well up on this subject, I can see. No. The Council probably don't have the powers, and in any case they are not too keen on a town-centre supermarket. We thought we were safe but then Roger got wind of what was going on, and from what I can tell, approached the developer and offered to act on their behalf with promises of influence within the Council, and over the Pottingers. Trevor heard on the grapevine that he had talked about a close friendship with us and that if the money was right, he was confident he could win us over. Iris confronted him with this. At first he denied any involvement and then said his firm acted for these people all over the Midlands and this was just another assignment. If sales are agreed, he would be doing the conveyancing, and that was all. I don't believe him; he's definitely more involved than that. Some share in the profits, I'm sure."

I listened attentively. Iris continued the story while Ambrose went to find some more ice. I was enjoying the malt.

"What infuriates us is that we are supposed to be friends and he never mentioned any of this until the agent told us he was involved. I know business is business, but he is supposed to be a lawyer and not a sort of site finder. He got quite aggressive when I told him we would not sell at any price. Very angry and seemed to insinuate I was just a woman who did not understand things."

"Well if you won't sell, surely you're safe."

"Yes. But it does leave a nasty taste. With both of them likely to be involved, I wanted him to stand down as the Director of *Private Lives*, but the old fool said that would be a retreat. Why should he give up something he loves so because Roger is being a shit."

"Do you think it is money? I always thought they were more than comfortable."

"Who knows? Let's talk about something else. How are you getting on with that reporter chap?"

"Oh, all right, but he is a bit immature."

Immature or not, I enrolled him into my investigation team and told him of the skulduggery Roger was said to be involved in. His first reaction was to say that surely all our leading man was doing was acting for clients who wished to purchase some property, assuming the owners are willing to sell. A naive point of view, I thought, but he promised to visit the Planning Department and see what he could discover. Fortunately, one of the junior officers in the Department is a leg break bowler of some skill: he had dismissed Adrian the week before for a paltry nine runs and so some useful inside information was obtained.

Adrian met me that evening acting like a dog returning a ball to its owner who had just hurled it one hundred yards into the long wet grass. He started to gambol even before ordering me a drink, for which sin he was suitably admonished.

"Evidently this supermarket chain has a bit of a reputation for sharp practice. A lifetime's supply of tea for the Mayor's mistress, that sort of thing, and even the occasional offshore bank account, but that's only gossip. Although the officers are not too keen the Deputy Chair of the Planning Committee seems to be in favour. Very left wing. Her ambition is to source cheap food for the workers. From all accounts she does not like Roger, not her type at all, but someone has seen a draft application that contains some socialist claptrap written by Roger to support Rosa Luxemburg and persuade her to begin talking about a possible compulsory purchase."

Rosa Luxemburg? Adrian has got the bit between his teeth.

"But why would Roger do that. I hate the man, but can hardly believe he would get involved in such a thing. It's simply not in his nature."

At the next rehearsal after the evening with the Pottingers, Roger was delayed in his office and Jeremy had been reading both men's parts but Brenda was there; some technical matter to discuss with Ambrose. I left the rehearsal with her when she commented that our ebullient Director had not seemed to be on form tonight.

"Most unlike Ambrose. Is he sickening for something, I wonder."

What an opening I thought.

"Yes. I think he is. I believe he and Iris are very agitated that someone is trying to persuade them to sell Pottingers and that Roger is involved."

"Goodness gracious. He's the lawyer for United Estates. Has been for years."

"But I was told there is some connection with that extraordinary woman on the Council. A sort illegitimate granddaughter of Karl Marx it is said."

Brenda paused.

"Well, May. It is frankly no business of yours, but there is nothing shameful going on. She is very eccentric, I grant, but her only motive is to help the poor. In Lloyd's Bank you do not see too many of the impecunious of Great Selsdon. Have you ever been to that council estate between here and Haddon? It's becoming as bad as the Glasgow Gorbals used to be."

Very well, I thought, but why is Roger involved? A possible answer to this question came from an unlikely source. As usual I met with Dave Littleton, the landlord of the Bull and Chairman of the Investment Club, two days before the September meeting to look at the results. We seemed to be doing very well and Dave was rather pleased about this; he did a lot of the stock picking.

"What are the rules about precipitate withdrawals?"

"I'm not sure. I'm only the typist."

"Had a call from Brenda Scotland. She wants out asap."

"Should you be telling me this?"

"Well, you're the Secretary. A bit short, she said, but I heard her precious husband has an unfortunate propensity for picking the wrong horse, or turning over the wrong card."

"I don't believe it. Roger Scotland, a gambler."

"That's what I'm told, but you know what this place is like for gossip. Probably Brenda just wants to buy a new car."

Was this the motive for the Pottinger affair? Our paragons are short of money.

Chapter Seven

The Dress Rehearsal

NEITHER THE tensions between Ambrose and the Scotlands, nor the differences between Ruth and Jeremy, should have had any impact on the technical side of the production, unless Brenda's involvement as the Stage Manager was affected by any possible financial crisis within her household. However, as is usually the case, no one could have foreseen how many problems would arise at the Technical Rehearsal, never mind what happened thereafter.

Perhaps I should explain what is involved in such a rehearsal. A check list might read as follows. Is the set properly constructed? Are the costumes complete? Has the lighting plot been agreed and are the lights in good working order? Are all the properties assembled and the curtain mechanics working? Has the lady in charge of make-up arrived? Is the 'Front of House' function organised – and the bar arranged and fully manned?

Quite straightforward, but not always so. Typical examples. No one has seen the make-up box since the last play. One of the doors on the set has no door knob. Three productions ago the drinks were safely locked away in the bar but the supplier of glasses failed to show; wrong date in the diary evidently. In fact, as I think back, the technicalities and all the other non-acting matters involved in staging a play, at least in the amateur field, are invariably beset by a host of errors and mishaps.

We never did successfully serve the food in *Separate Tables*. Reliable Joan cooked something new every day of the four performances but more of it invariably finished up on the floor, or in the laps of the performers, then stayed on the plates. It was not until the last night that we partially solved the problem by gluing the plates to the tables. However, we could not so attach the Shepherd's Pie or the Beef Goulash in a similar manner and however hard the food-spattered actors tried, there were still complaints from the spectators on the front row who did not appreciate cold mince being mixed with their boxes of Cadbury's Milk Tray or Terry's Old Gold.

The broken main fuse that occurred during the last night of *Ring Around the Moon* could not have been foreseen but the rogue spotlight that focussed on Mr Winslow Senior picking his nose did not add to the gravitas of that particular play. Add to these concerns the countless catastrophes with the curtains and you can understand how essential a run-through of technical matters is.

Those curtains. The least of the problems is to have them open and unable to close; at least the set and actors are then on view, but if stuck halfway so that the inter-play between Jack and Algy is played out on a piece of stage only three feet wide, Lane of course is invisible, is only mildly disastrous compared to them being incapable of any movement whatsoever. When this occurred, as happened more than once, Ambrose from backstage could be heard throughout the Hall with the result that everyone is privy to his views on the probability that the Stage Manager had unknown parents and that the Director is about to retire to Eastbourne, because those wretched curtains are stuck in the closed position.

For *Private Lives*, there was one administrative item that had not been dealt with. Brenda asked Ambrose if the little matter of obtaining a licence to present this play had been obtained from the guardians of Mr Coward's copyright. Unfortunately I was nearby when this question was asked.

"Of course, Madam Stage Manager. At least I assume so."

"Well, Ambrose, it is quite important. We could be in trouble if we have not paid. The Master would turn in his grave."

"May, I presume you've dealt with this?"

"No Ambrose, I thought, the Director was responsible, or the Treasurer?"

"Yes, of course. Jackson will have seen to it."

Nothing else was said but I had a bet with myself that Jack-off was most unlikely to have been that efficient, particularly as for this play he had been busy with Publicity. I won my wager. When I spoke to him he was rather abrupt; perhaps understandably so, and said it was not his job.

I thought back. Surely in the past, one of the first things the Director did before the play was even cast was to obtain copies of French's Acting Edition of the contemplated work and pay to Samuel French, or whomever, the requisite fee for permission for an amateur group to stage this particular work, for four nights only. In these Acting Editions is printed, in bold type, the words: 'The fee must be paid, and a licence obtained, before a performance is given'.

Ambrose had done this many times; it should have been automatic. He really was not himself. I found out what the current cost was, got Jackson to give me a cheque and when the licence arrived I filed it away with the official minutes of the Society's Committee meetings.

Definitely not up to the mark. He never mentioned again the conversation with Brenda – did not even seem to think about it – but that minor irregularity was not really serious whereas Ambrose's next move was, and where he was guilty of a serious error of judgement. He was so proud of the blossoming of Alison, and ignoring any tensions surrounding his other three players, he declared that the acting side of our play was as near perfect as could be and so, with such an excellent Stage Manager as Brenda, the Technical Rehearsal and the Dress Rehearsal would be combined as a single event.

Many of us were concerned about this, but said nothing. Fortunately Brenda did.

"Ambrose. We always have a final Technical Rehearsal separate from the Dress."

"Yes, my dear. But my little cast are so perfect all they have to do is to turn up on stage wearing their beautiful costumes and expertly made up by the joyful Janice."

"But, if on the night there is no tray of cocktails for Amanda to bring on, it will be devastating, however good an actress she is."

Having made his decision, Ambrose was reluctant to back down but as a compromise, and with everyone's begrudging acquiescence, it was agreed that in addition to the combined Dress and Technical rehearsal on the Tuesday – we were playing as usual from Wednesday to Saturday – we would have a complete run through of the play, with props but no costumes or make-up, on the Monday night. Many grumbled, including me as I had arranged a rendezvous with Adrian, but I think we all sensed that this production was going to be a resounding success – an excellent cast and with Brenda pulling the strings back stage – so we were prepared to put in that little extra.

Monday came. It had been raining all day and seemed to get heavier as we assembled. Gum boots, umbrellas and wet mackintoshes did nothing to persuade anyone that we were in Coward country and certainly none of us felt in the jubilant mood displayed by our foolish and optimistic maestro. Ruth said she thought she was developing shingles and Eric told all who would listen that he wished he was sheltering from the weather in the snug at the Bull rather than listening to the ebullient Ambrose. Despite the fact that but for him I would have been at the Green Man at Lower Marston with my reporter friend, at the Village Hall he was absent; some emergency with a car crash on the A16. Joan had telephoned that delivery of some of the props was delayed due to a flat tyre and I could see the black circles observed of late around Brenda's eyes were darkening by the minute. And then I had to drive Alison back to her mother's house to collect the left shoe she had omitted to bring with her: Ambrose would not allow her on stage other than in high heels and so, I thought, the ingredients for a dismal evening were assembling before his very eyes.

At first, he did not see them, although he could not avoid Ruth's shrieks of anguish when she observed spots of white paint decorating the piano for which she felt herself responsible. For Act One this instrument should not have been on view but those two incompetent stage-hands, Simon and Monica, had been putting into place the ingenious cover conceived by Brenda and built by Eric when it fell apart.

Not Eric's fault. It was not constructed so that one side could be moved in an easterly direction while the other was pulled to the west as a result of which those idiot scene-shifters were left with a piece in each hand. This meant that the top was then precariously perched on the piano, adding even more cries of distress from an already distraught Ruth. Eric assured her that it was only emulsion paint that could easily be cleaned away but I do not think his remarks gave her any comfort. Like all of us she was cold and tending towards the shivering state, brought on by the room temperature and the fear of an impending disaster.

Ambrose ignored all of this as the piano cover, in three sections, was moved out of sight to be severely dealt with by the ubiquitous hammer and nails.

"Right everyone. Let's first check the curtains. Brenda. Please close them."

"No, all the way. We do not want the audience to catch a glimpse of your wonderful set until the music begins."

"Well, why are they stuck? Press the button with more vigour."

"All right. Try it manually. Pull hard."

"Good. Now, opening music please."

"Well, who said he could take the tape recorder home with him? And why is he not here yet?"

"I don't care if he is reporting on the sinking of the Titanic, I want the music."

"No Roger. It will not suffice if you play the piano."

"May. Get that Adrian, what's his name, here pronto. Take a break everyone while I look at the props."

"Props. Where are the baguettes? A sliced loaf will not do."

"Where is the window for the last two acts?"

"Sam. There are two bulbs missing in the footlights."

"Keep the noise down."

"Alison, my dear. Why are you wearing odd shoes?"

"Ruth. You are distressed. We can clean the piano I'm sure. Chicken pox. Oh dear, I hope not. Beechams and hot lemon tonight and a large dollop of Scotch."

"Roger. I think it is too early for alcoholic stimulants even if you do say they are essential on a night like this."

Ambrose is finally beginning to accept the true state of affairs, and as a result his first tantrum was directed at me as a result of the absence of Adrian. Why should I be blamed? I am not his keeper but I was well aware that the amateur dramatic bug had not bitten this young man like the rest of us gathered together in this dismal venue. In keeping with the weather, the central heating seemed to be performing as poorly as our extra rehearsal.

There had been a second sampling by Roger of the spirit he kept in his silver hip flask before the tape recorder and its operative had arrived but this did coincide with Sam being able to replace the defective fuse that had disabled the curtain mechanism.

"Right. Let's go. Music and curtain up."

You can guess what happened next. Adrian, out of breath and no doubt somewhat ruffled by the words I had directed at him, pressed the wrong button and the curtains opened onto two sweet little terraces at that fated French hotel to the strains of *Some Enchanted Evening* which was part of the interval music assembled by Vera. This included a selection from the *Wizard of Oz* and, curiously, *South Pacific*.

As the night wore on Ambrose did become nearly speechless but at this early stage he was in full possession of his vocal chords.

"Close the curtains. That's not Coward music. What is going on? Is this deliberate sabotage? Is my triumph to be shattered by some nincompoop who is out of sight?"

He had a script in his hand at this point, at least until it bounced off my head, and so I vowed, for the rest of the evening, to keep as far away from our Director as possible. The strains of *Someday I'll Find You* replaced *Some Enchanted Evening* as the curtains slowly opened, with pride it would seem, but the piano cover was not in place; repairs were taking longer than expected and we could all hear the hammers still at work.

"What's the piano there for? This is Act One."

Brenda explained and suggested the actors begin with the exposed piano but Ambrose stopped the action when Roger, accidentally on purpose, ran his fingers along the keys of the instrument as he made his entrance. Brenda was not enjoying the evening but her husband clearly was. As long as he was given, in due course, the opportunity to shine as the elegant and amusing Elyot, in all his glory, he could relish Ambrose's discomfort like tasting a glass of Chateau Haut Brion 1995.

The same was not true of Jeremy and I was certainly beginning to see him in a new light. He appeared to be genuinely concerned about Ruth's distress over the piano and her incipient malady, and I thought at one moment he was going to give Roger a lecture on how to behave like a gentleman. Ruth tried her best to project Amanda across the footlights but she was not helped by the fact that Sam had not yet managed to direct his spotlight on her, designed as it was to highlight that crucial line.

AMANDA:Darling, I daren't, it's too wicked of us, I simply daren't.

You will, I am sure, be asking how these errors were occurring with the experienced and efficient Brenda as the Stage Manager. Was she distracted by external events that were uppermost in her mind so that *Private Lives* did not have the prominence it should, or could have, compared with what was agitating her; whatever that was? I was no nearer the truth. Financial problems? Roger's legal or illegal activities? Or was she concerned about the health or behaviour of one of her children?

Whatever, Ambrose was not getting the backstage expertise he deserved. He had worked hard with his cast. His choice of Alison had not been the disaster predicted and, in fact, I was beginning to see her as quite the equal of the two men even though at the moment Roger appeared to be emulating Nero as Rome burned. He had seen the emergence of technical problems in previous productions but in one way or another they were always solved, or partly so, in time for him to make his entrance on opening night. This would surely be the case with *Private Lives* but until then he revelled in Ambrose's discomfort. Eventually he would be on stage, immaculately dressed and groomed, ready to overshadow Alison/Sibyl and reduce her to the silly girl he considered she was in real life: and also ready to expose Ruth as an inadequate Amanda in comparison to the portrait his own wife would have given if that pompous little prick Pottinger had not been involved.

But none of this came about. After more than two hours of ironing out the technical difficulties, two hours that had wreaked havoc with his temperament, Ambrose was finally able to show the assembled members of the Society his quartet of perfectly rehearsed actors, ready to go and play their parts. But, no one could have imagined that the problems of the night were only just beginning.

"At last everyone. Places please. Music. Curtain, and good luck to you all."

It was not altogether Ambrose's fault. Perhaps because of the delay, or the weather, Roger, for once, allowed his arrogance to overpower his talent and I could see that the first scene with Sibyl was not right; he was moving into dangerous waters and I believe even Alison realised something was amiss. Let me take you through a part of it.

ELYOT: I was wondering what was going on inside your mind, what your plans are really?
SIBYL:Plans; Oh Elli!
ELYOT:Apart from loving me and all that, you must have plans.
SIBYL:I haven't the faintest idea what you're talking about.
ELYOT:Perhaps it's subconscious then, age old instincts working away deep down, mincing up little bits of experience for future use, watching me carefully like a sharp-eyed blonde kitten.
SIBYL:How can you be so horrid.
ELYOT:I said Kitten, not Cat.
SIBYL:Kittens grow into cats.
ELYOT:Let that be a warning to you.

SIBYL:You're very strange all of a sudden, and rather cruel. Just because I'm feminine. It doesn't mean that I'm crafty and calculating.
ELYOT:I didn't say you were either of those things.
SIBYL:I hate these half-masculine women who go banging about.
ELYOT:I hate anybody who goes banging about.

"Stop, Roger. This is the first sign of the rather nasty Elyot emerging. Please make him so."

Roger continued in an even more lethargic and supercilious manner.

"My dear fellow. 'Banging about' is of course funny but you cannot be entirely laid-back and languid. This is the time when you are indicating, in a subtle way, that you are on honeymoon with a girl who you are not passionately in love with. A little more condescending I believe. Go back to 'Perhaps it's subconscious'."

Elyot returned to the line Ambrose indicated, but did not change his apathetic manner one iota.

"No. I won't have it. You have it wrong. There has to be a change of emphasis. Please concentrate, Roger."

Our star scowled and carried on but it was clear that by this time Ambrose was becoming tired and irritable. It had been a long evening thanks to combining the Technical Rehearsal with an acting run-through.

"Stop. Mr Scotland, you have not got it. Behaving more like a ham than usual."

"What did you say?"

Ambrose repeated the sentence using a series of different words but I believe they still included the one spelt HAM. Roger smouldered. I am sure I saw smoke framing his exquisitely Brylcreemed coiffeur.

"How dare you. I will not take that from an insignificant ponce like you."

Brenda appeared from the wings and gently prevented her husband from jumping over the footlights, but nevertheless we could all see his blazing eyes and clenched fists.

"A ham. I have never been so insulted in my life. You've gone too far this time. You can stuff your Coward up his arse. And up yours too. Elyot is making a final exit. Your *Private Lives* is over. It is in ruins. You have only one and a half couples, but I'm sure a genius Director like you will be able to explain my absence to your shitty audience. And you can be your own Stage Manager. Brenda leaves with me."

Bizarrely, he then turned towards Alison.

"You remember the first rehearsal, you stupid creature, when you wondered if you would be called upon to kiss me? Well, just this once."

He then seized her round that elegant neck, kissed her long and passionately and then, as he released her, his hands strayed over the bosoms that Doreen's rehearsal gown had been unable to repress. Brenda stood with her mouth open, but then smiled as though she understood what was happening, even if at that stage she did not believe Roger was about to give up his Elyot. But he was. He took Brenda by the hand, kissed her as well, and our Richard Burton and Elizabeth Taylor exited Stage Left before another word was uttered.

For some reason Adrian thought some music might be appropriate, or did he again just press a button by mistake. Whatever, the hall was suddenly filled with the strains of *I'm Gonna Wash That Man Right Outa My Hair*. As an accompaniment to what we had just witnessed, it could not have been bettered.

Why had this crisis only arisen at this last moment? Was Roger being deliberately difficult, or was Ambrose letting his dislike of our Elyot come to the boil at this time of all times, forty eight hours before curtain-up, without fully understanding the possible consequences? Or could it be dismissed under the heading of 'that's amateur dramatics for you'. No matter what, I was most concerned about Ambrose. He had seated himself with a blank look on his face, but even more worrying that face was now pale and not puce. Except for the canned orchestra there was absolute silence in the auditorium, only broken as we heard the rear door close with a bang. Two days before the curtain went up we had no Elyot, and no Stage Manager. A very disenchanted evening.

As this was a pre-Dress Rehearsal, some members of the Society not involved in this particular production were there to witness what had become a dramatic fiasco of the first water. Amongst these were Helen and George. No one moved, or said anything, as they walked, in step, from the back of the hall and stood either side of the hapless Ambrose, where they began whispering into his ears. I can imagine what was being said. Expressions of sympathy: what a cad Roger was: sorry Brenda had to be involved: what a disaster: what is to be done. Helen would be offering to print, first thing on the morrow, notices that could be distributed around the town alerting our paying customers to the fact that due to unforeseen circumstances, the Society's production of *Private Lives* was cancelled; and a full refund would be made available if ticket holders would visit Pottinger's

Travel Agency or contact any member of the committee excluding, I assumed, our Chairman. Who would be detailed to relay the news to him I wondered? Also, could Adrian and Eustace Simpson produce an emergency issue of *The Record* with news of the cancellation? What a scoop for them.

Or was there an alternative? The diminutive Ambrose would take over Elyot and read the part. What would that do, I conjectured, for Alison's composure. Mad idea crowded on mad idea. A performance of *Private Lives* without an Elyot? No, not possible. Jeremy to play both parts wearing a coloured wig when representing Elyot – after all, they are not on stage together until the entrance at the end of Act Two – but then of course by Act Three my plot is exposed. Delay opening night while a substitute is found; but whom? Or should we all take an early Christmas break and run away from Great Selsdon before we are burnt at the stake, in the Market Square, by the furious ticket holders. On the other hand, perhaps they would be glad of an excuse not to venture from their firesides on a wet and cold autumn night, rain and sleet were forecast for the weekend, just to see those Scotland's farting around in their usual show-off manner.

No one could have guessed the true subject of the conversation between our Director and the Thurston Browns but whatever it was I could see some colour coming back into Ambrose's cheeks. He motioned the three remaining principals and Eric to join him, which they did. After a few moments Jeremy put his arm around George's shoulder, patted him on the back and kissed Helen. Ruth was giggling but Alison looked vague. Ambrose began to bounce about on his toes as he called everyone on to the stage. By the look on his face the bending of the knees on this occasion clearly presaged an item of pleasure rather than rage or despair.

"Ladies and gentlemen. Boys and girls. In the words of whomever, 'The show must go on'."

He paused. We listened to this cliché with little enthusiasm, but Ambrose was nothing if not quick witted.

"Those of you who are as fond of Mr Coward as I am will know that he wrote a satirical song called *Why Must The Show Go On*. He makes fun of such sentiments but in the circumstances I believe he would applaud our determination to persevere and present his marvellous play."

I could not understand what was happening but he was grinning like the proverbial Cheshire Cat.

"I take all the blame. I shall probably be sued for slander by Roger Scotland. He is a ham, although I should not have told him so at this particular juncture. But, I confess, from the outset I wanted Jeremy to be my Elyot, and yours too my good people, but I could not get my way. The Roger effect was too strong, and I must tell you our dear Chairman was keen for Mr Scotland to be awarded this part. Jeremy has played Elyot before. He assures me he is word perfect and therefore we have a ready-made substitute for the precious Roger. So let's hear it for Mr Jeremy Coxon."

There was an attempt by some present to clap, in a desultory manner, but all saw the flaw. Even Alison registered the fact. If Jeremy is now Elyot, who is to play Victor?

"Some of you may be unaware of the close interest Helen Thurston Brown has in the Players. Very close. We need her on the Committee".

At that juncture I am sure I heard, sotto voce, the words 'potential new Chairman'.

"George and Jeremy have not, of recent times, been the best of friends. Other matters. Nothing to do with George being passed over as Victor but whatever he has been encouraged by his clever wife to learn the lines of the character he wanted to play and he tells me he has done so. Helen has not spoken to me on this subject, wanted to leave me free to concentrate on the arduous task of directing this masterpiece, but she has been worried for some time that there were no stand-ins for such a small cast and that one withdrawal would be ruinous. So, she and George have spent these dark evenings reading the play together and learning not only the part of Victor but Amanda as well. Brilliant. If our new star, Miss Street, had been run over by a bus, or fallen from a motor cycle, Ruth could have stood in for Sibyl and the clever Mrs Thurston Brown could become Amanda. Similarly, if Ruth had been injured with a hockey stick being wielded by one of her enthusiastic girls, Helen is at hand."

I could see the confidence returning to Ambrose. It was coursing through his veins alongside the blood that was bringing colour back to his chubby cheeks as the grin on his face widened. Adrian pressed another button and we all laughed as the strains of *Happy Talk* spread around the hall. Another mistake, or was he more adept than I give him credit for. Ambrose went on.

"The other good news is that I have promised Eric that I will do my best to find him a part in our next production to reward him for volunteering to take over as the Stage Manager."

It must be one of the Mechanicals; Bottom at least I thought.

"It has been a long and fraught night. I want everyone here tomorrow by 6pm for the Dress Rehearsal. Ruth tells me she can find another teacher to take games tomorrow afternoon so we can have an intense meeting of the cast from 1 p.m. and May, you'll have to call in sick as we are going to need a first class prompt."

When Adrian left me at my door even he could see the glow I had – not from the obvious admiration he displayed at all my charms but because of the promotion in status accorded by Ambrose's last statement. 'A first class prompt'. I rather looked forward to the next day. Success or disaster.

I decided not to call in sick. My manager had tickets for the first night of the play and I explained that a minor problem had arisen and that Mr Pottinger needed my services for that Tuesday afternoon and could I please be excused. If things went well, I might be back at the bank before it was time for cashing up, but in any case, I was sure the other staff could manage without me. In the event they did need to cope without my help; it was a very long afternoon.

Before the new Victor made an appearance, Helen had already raided her husband's wardrobe and made some judicious extra purchasers at Marshalls, the Gentleman's Outfitter, so George appeared reasonably attired in the garb of Coward's man. Jeremy, under his own steam, seemed to have been able to transform his Victor costume into one worthy of Elyot Chase so Doreen's intervention became minimal; just a new coloured handkerchief for the top pocket of the tweed jacket.

The major problem of course was going to be the moves. Provided there are no pregnant pauses (why this adjective I wonder) in the dialogue, the theatregoer is not too concerned if there are mistakes in the spoken word but if Amanda directs remarks to Victor, and he is not on stage, such a bloomer can lead to hoots of derision.

Jeremy knew when Elyot should appear or exit but it was all new to George, the moves in Act Three being the major problem. In the first Act, Ruth was splendid. By a touch of the elbow or a raising of the eyebrows she was able to arrange Victor's entrances and exits with a minimum of hesitations.

Getting on and off the stage at the correct moment is naturally an essential of the actor's art. Exits are not normally a problem; if someone is disinclined to leave the stage the other actors can usually indicate to the hesitant one that he or she needs to depart – unless it is a Hamlet soliloquy where he is alone on the stage and does not move until someone enters to precipitate a delayed exit by the Prince. The more serious problem in the amateur world is the entrance.

One of the worst examples in my experience involved the efficient and reliable Mr Ready. It was not entirely his fault. Janice can be a little giddy at times.

Owen, as Dr Chasuble, makes his first entrance to find Miss Prism hard at work tutoring her reluctant pupil Cecily. The subject is German grammar which holds no delight for the young lady who considers that she becomes positively plain when speaking German. This leads on to a discussion about three volume novels and then Canon Chasuble appears on the scene, much to the pleasure of Miss Prism and the delight of Cecily who spies a prospective diversion from her loathsome lessons.

But, on the second night of our production, the clergyman failed to appear. It was difficult for Tricia, playing Miss Prism, to cover for the Canon's non-appearance because of Cecily's line: 'But I see Dr Chasuble coming up through the garden.' At this Miss Prism has to rise from her seat but when she realises that there is no one to greet, Tricia sat down again and looked blankly at Cecily. Unfortunately she was not experienced enough to avoid the pause painfully obvious to the audience, and Ambrose, but when she did gather her wits together she shrugged her shoulders and instructed Cecily to continue with her German revision. This did not help much because the girl did exactly that and picked up her textbook without saying a word. Tricia tried. Told her charge that the Canon must have been delayed and then wondered why. By this time Eric had found the absent Owen and pushed him, with some force, on to the stage where he was able to pick up the dialogue with the two ladies as though nothing was amiss.

As can be imagined Ambrose was most upset and very disappointed that Owen had let him down. But what was the reason? It was romance, of a sort, although not exactly Mills and Boon or the subject of a blue movie.

I have not yet to talked about illicit love affairs, another of the hazards of amateur theatre. I use the words, 'love affairs' in their widest sense from the divorce proceedings that came about after the female Aladdin formed a passionate attachment to the rather handsome fellow, I cannot recall his name, who was playing the front half of a camel to a mild and innocent dalliance that never proceeds beyond the occasional stolen kiss. Mostly these engagements occur within the acting fraternity: appearing as Casanova or a notorious femme fatale tends to remove inhibitions and, like the drunken headmaster, there is some inclination to continue their roles in the field of love, after the makeup has been removed, using the stage door or behind the curtains in the wings as locales for their antics, however active or passive they might be.

I may have already shown Janice to be somewhat volatile and I regret to say that this characteristic was at its height during the Wilde play. The chap playing Jack took rather a shine to Owen's wife, who as usual was in charge of makeup, and she was rather flattered. In fact, I think she encouraged him. On that second night, Canon Chasuble had been outside to smoke a cigarette before his entrance but when he returned to the dressing room to check that his dog collar was in place he found his wife in a close embrace with Mr Worthing where she was using her lips and tongue to seriously damage the makeup she had applied to those pallid cheeks only two hours before. Owen later blamed her behaviour on the extra glass of gin she had drunk that evening but at the time of discovery he could only find guilty the young man who detached himself from Janice in double quick time: but not speedily enough to avoid the boot up the backside administered by the cuckolded husband. What made it worse was that Janice showed no shame and simply laughed out loud at her two lovers. This sent Jack scampering away but added two more vital minutes to Owen's absence from the stage as he tried to avoid joining in with Janice's hilarity.

To the best of my knowledge we had no backstage sex scandals in *Private Lives* but to return to that afternoon rehearsal, George was, as promised, word perfect in the Victor role. I was amazed. Helen is a magician. He even managed to add his ability as a pipe smoker to the new member of the quartet. Without any instructions from Ambrose, or objections by him, he used his briar to wag at Amanda as he refused to leave their honeymoon hotel at her say so. I think even Jeremy was impressed with George's delivery of the line:

I'm not going to leave, Mandy. If I start giving into you as early as this, our lives will be unbearable.

– emphasised by the flapping pipe.

Except for the silent and dramatic appearance of Victor, with Sibyl, at the end of Act Two, his main involvement in the play comes in Act Three. The substitutes for the two men found the first Act not too difficult; Jeremy soon found his feet in the crucial scene with Amanda and, as I have said, in the same Act Ruth was able to ensure that Victor was more or less in the right place at the right time. Ambrose quickly realised this and so he spent most of that Monday afternoon on Act Three converting Jeremy from a Victor to an Elyot and introducing George to the character of Victor.

Jeremy is smart. If Roger's desertion becomes a long-term affair perhaps there is another leading man waiting in the wings: and another Brenda in Ruth? Who can tell? Whatever, it was predictable that however quick-witted, there were occasions when Jeremy was tempted to deliver both Elyot and Victor's lines – but Ambrose soon smoothed that out.

"Jeremy. I know it's difficult, but you have to give George a chance to respond. This is, after all, his first rehearsal. Let's try it again from where they seem to be ready to fight each other. George, this has to be brisk."

ELYOT: Certainly. I'll take back anything, if only you'll stop bellowing at me.
VICTOR [contemptuously]: You're a coward too.
ELYOT: They want us to fight, don't you see?
VICTOR: No. I don't, why should they?

ELYOT:Primitive feminine instincts – warring males – very enjoyable.
VICTOR: You think you're very clever, don't you?
ELYOT:I think I'm a bit cleverer than you, but apparently that's not saying much.
VICTOR [violently]: What?
ELYOT: Oh, do sit down.
VICTOR: I will not.
ELYOT:Well, if you'll excuse me, I will; I'm extremely tired.
[He sits down.
VICTOR:Oh, for God's sake, behave like a man.

ELYOT:Now if you'll explained to me satisfactorily how all that can possibly improve the situation, I'll tear off my coat, and we'll go at one another hammer and tongs, immediately.
VICTOR:It would ease my mind.
ELYOT:Only if you won.
VICTOR:I should win all right.
ELYOT:Want to try?
VICTOR:Yes.
ELYOT: [jumping up] Here goes then–
[He tears off his coat.
VICTOR:Just a moment.
ELYOT:Well?
VICTOR:What did you mean about them wanting us to fight?
ELYOT:It would be balm to their vanity.

"Jeremy. When Elyot is provoked into standing up and he takes off his coat, I think you both know what this scene is about. Victor is a bit of a bully but it's the classic situation of a belligerent pair that threaten each other but neither intends it to come to fisticuffs."

"Of course Ambrose" Jeremy replied, "and it is interesting that such behaviour stands in direct contrast to the females who do not hesitate to precipitate real violence."

By the end of the rehearsal George was picking up the cues reasonably well but, as you might expect, the quick fire repartee that Roger and Jeremy had perfected could not be repeated, although

I did think the one improvement on the original was that George looked more like my image of Victor.

As I've said, George was word perfect, and Jeremy soon got his tongue around the Elyot lines rather than those of Victor, but let us reflect and put this into context. George had woken up with the thought that in the evening he and Helen were going to observe Ambrose at work conducting nearly the last rehearsal of *Private Lives* before the real thing, and then by the end of that day he was part of that real thing. With Jeremy, as he made his approach shot to the 18th green before lunch he could have had no idea that before he laid his head on the pillow that night he would be Elyot and not Victor. I can only describe the outcome as a miracle. It would overall have been a slicker production, a more polished presentation, if Roger had not defected but George and Jeremy did so well, it was a triumph of a different nature.

There had not been an opportunity for me to discuss these totally unexpected changes with either Alison or Ruth but I suspect they were both in favour. Roger's snide remarks had impacted little on the younger of these two ladies; and probably she did not really understand the irony of his farewell kiss. She told me later he was a surprisingly 'good kisser' but I guessed she was going to find Jeremy easier to work with at the beginning of the play. On the other hand, the final physical engagement with Victor would need to be toned down as her opponent was the older and less mobile George. Ambrose was on to that minor difficulty at an early stage and devoted time to explaining matters to Alison.

"Now, Sibyl. The last altercation with Victor. I know you liked dishing out the punishment to Jeremy, but my dear girl you must be more gentle with Mr Thurston Brown. He does not know the action as you do. You must reduce the power in that final slap. We need him for all four nights you know."

Alison indicated that she understood this and ruffled George's hair. He looked rather pleased at this and decided to light his pipe again.

"George. I like the way Victor has now become a pipe smoker but please use judiciously. We do not want our delightful ladies to be rendered invisible by a smokescreen of your making."

I concentrated on the script, prompting Jeremy and George as they went astray, but my mind was racing to imagine what was happening in the Scotland household. Ambrose had told Trevor of what had occurred the evening before knowing that news of the miraculous rescue by the Thurston Browns would thereby have been communicated to Roger. Would he buy a ticket hoping to see the botched-up version that *Private Lives* was forced to be without him, or had they both already left for a few days in the real Paris leaving behind a wet and dark autumn at the Village Hall? Could they afford Paris? Were any regrets emerging yet? Did Brenda fully support his stance?

It was she I felt sorry for. Brenda had accepted Ruth being given the part she wanted and even if she was angry and annoyed with Ambrose, she and Iris had been close friends for many years and I am sure that as far as the Players as a whole were concerned, it was not in her nature to ruin a production in this way. I recalled how she had continued with Ruth Condomine in *Blithe Spirit* after breaking her arm.

For some reason I called to mind the headmaster and *Educating Rita*. The dipsomania had eventually been brought under control but had Roger acted in the way he had because he had so imbibed the character of Elyot to become totally selfish, thoughtless and uncaring. Or is Roger that anyway? Elyot Chase may be charming and handsome and witty, but he's not a very nice man, is he? Amanda is just as thoughtless and Sibyl rather silly, but I would not want to fall in love with an Elyot. Amanda deserts Victor, but who is mainly to blame? Elyot.

AMANDA:I do hope you met a sacred elephant. They're lint white I believe, and very, very sweet.
ELYOT:I've never loved anyone else for an instant.
AMANDA [raising her hand feebly in protest]: No, no, you mustn't –
Elyot – stop.
ELYOT:You love me, too, don't you? There's no doubt about it anywhere, is there?
AMANDA:No, no doubt anywhere.

AMANDA:We must think quickly, oh quickly
ELYOT:Escape?
AMANDA:Together?
ELYOT:Yes, of course, now, now.
AMANDA:We can't, we can't, you know we can't.
ELYOT:We must.
AMANDA:It would break Victor's heart.

I have already made it clear that I have never liked Roger Scotland, but am I being altogether fair and impartial? He is a good actor, and I believe a good family man and father, and he has never walked out on a production before – but then you might consider Ambrose's attitude and his injudicious use of the word 'ham' justifies this current action. But, has the dreaded lurgy struck again? The selfish Elyot walked out on Sibyl on their honeymoon without a second's thought just as Roger has deserted the Players. In both cases these actions display identical egos, out of control, with no thought for anyone else. Elyot pays no heed to the distress he causes Sibyl and Victor. It is what he wants. No one else matters and thanks to Mr Coward's talent in creating such a monster, the diabolical Roger appears to have become the Benedict Arnold – or is it the Frankenstein – of the Great Selsdon Amateur Dramatic Society.

What an introduction to the climax of my little tale.

Chapter Eight

The Performance

JACKSON, OUR indolent Treasurer, had done an amazingly good job with the publicity. One of Owen Ready's workers was a part-time artist, mostly pen and ink, and he had produced a striking piece of artwork of adjoining balconies that was used for the poster and the programme. Where Jack-off had done particularly well had been in persuading local businesses to advertise. Incredibly, he seemed to have been stung by Trevor's remarks, and no doubt by the rather nasty trick I had played, to pull out all the stops so that the final programme was well fattened out by twenty page of advertisements, all at £100 each.

But of course, by the time of the Dress Rehearsal this splendidly printed document was inaccurate. I took the initiative and drafted, for Ambrose's approval, the erratum slip that would need to be prepared to register the changes.

At the eleventh hour, Mr Roger Scotland has decided he did not wish to perform the role of Elyot Chase and so he and his wife, Brenda Scotland, will not be participating in our Twenty-fifth Anniversary production of *Private Lives*. Mr Jeremy Coxon, who was scheduled to play Victor Prynne, will take over the lead role with the part of Victor to be played by George Thurston Brown. Eric Winstanley is the Stage Manager.

Ambrose dismissed my words out of hand and what the audience will read as they open up their programmes is the following, printed on a strip of white paper of good quality, courtesy of Spire Printing.

Due to the unavailability of Mr and Mrs Scotland, Jeremy Coxon will now be playing Elyot Chase, George Thurston Brown, Victor Prynne and Eric Winstanley is the Stage Manager.

Eric had no difficulties with stepping into Brenda's shoes; and I cannot resist adding, 'provided the heels were not too high'. He had been the Stage Manager many times in the past and I think he might be more able than Brenda to deal with the inefficient Adrian and his mischievous machine but, on the acting side, the first thing I have to say is that there was one clear winner resulting from Roger's defection, and that was Ruth. If she had the same opinion of him as I did, she never expressed such a view, but alongside the new Elyot she blossomed like a spring flower appearing as if by magic from the cold winter earth. She had done well playing against, or with Roger, where she made an impressive attempt to match his brio, particularly in the fracas at the end of Act Two, but with Jeremy she appeared lighter, even frivolous and yet strong at the same time.

Early in the play Elyot tells Sibyl that Amanda is 'marked for tragedy – bound to make a mess of everything' but as the action progresses, and as Ruth portrays her, this only goes to show how trite and unperceptive is Coward's Elyot because Amanda is so much more in control of events than her partner: she does not make a mess of things and is no tragedienne. I speculated whether Brenda would have conveyed this or am I judging the stage Amanda against the respective characters of Roger's wife and Ruth; or at least my interpretation of their characters. In my view, Brenda's persona has to be tainted by the failings of her husband compared with the innocence and goodness that I see in Ruth.

I would hesitate to air this opinion with anyone else – even if I was able to clearly explain myself – but by the end of a four night run it was manifest that I was not the only one who thought that Ruth was the star of the show. This was made evident at the curtain calls. With such a small cast, Ambrose gave each of the quartet an opportunity for an individual bow before all four returned together, with the maid hovering on the fringes, and on the last night a goodly portion of the audience stood to applaud our Amanda.

The other facet of her performance that seemed to blossom without Roger was the singing. Ambrose had worked hard on the scene where they realise they are occupying adjoining balconies and where this discovery comes about through music. The stage instructions are precise.

The orchestra downstairs strikes up a new melody. Both ELYOT *and* AMANDA *give a little start. After a moment,* ELYOT *pensively begins to hum the tune the band is playing. It is a sentimental, romantic little tune.* AMANDA *hears him, and clutches at her throat suddenly as though she were suffocating. Then she jumps up noiselessly, and peers over the line of tubs.* ELYOT, *with his back to her, continues to sing obliviously. She sits down again, relaxing with a gesture almost of despair. Then she looks anxiously over her shoulder at the window in case* VICTOR *should be listening, and then, with a little smile, she takes up the melody herself, clearly.* ELYOT *stops dead and gives a gasp, then he jumps up, and stands looking at her. She continues to sing, pretending not to know that he is there. At the end of the song, she turns slowly, and faces him.*

This of course is a crucial moment in the play. As Ambrose said, more than once, 'If music be the food of love, play on.' What the playwright does not determine is which piece of music should be used but Ambrose had followed tradition and chosen *Someday I'll Find You.* Ruth sang it most beautifully in a small clear voice that even made the heart of that experienced campaigner, May Twining, give a flutter or two. And one or two tears as Amanda herself exhibits when she reprises the song ten pages later.

Someday I'll find you,
Moonlight behind you,
True to the dream I am dreaming.
As I draw near you,
You'll smile a little smile,
For a little while,

142

We shall stand,
Hand in hand.
I'll leave you never,
Love you for ever,
All our past sorrow redeeming.
Try to make it true,
Say you love me too,
Someday I'll find you again.

It appeared that Alison had to some extent been impervious to Roger's view of her acting ability, mainly thanks to Ambrose's adroit guidance of the inexperienced girl, but when she had Jeremy and George as her partners, she showed, without realising it, that Roger had actually been an inhibiting factor. The individual applause she received was generous, perhaps dangerously so. I have talked about how the amateur theatre virus can attach itself to anyone but I had thought Alison was immune and if offered a stage part in the future would, 'take it or leave it.' But, it looked as though her experience as Coward's Sibyl was going to have a lasting effect. As she came into the wings, after listening to the appreciation of the audience that she had deservedly earned, I could see from the smile on her face that she was about to ask me if there was a role she might apply for in the next production. Playfully I was tempted to tell her we were planning *Journey's End* where all of the characters are soldiers, and male, but I was not that cruel.

Inevitably mistakes were made by the two men. Even if Jeremy could recall Elyot's words he needed to be very quick-witted to pick up all of the cue lines without hesitation and not make a hash of the moves. Fortunately, in this play, there are not too many. The ones on the balconies are fairly obvious and for most of Acts Two and Three the activity is one of languor rather than vigour, and so there were no real embarrassments on the Jeremy front.

George was of course totally new to the set and on each of the four nights he managed to collide with the large settee that is such a feature of the furnishings for the last two Acts. Not always at the same moment each evening but while striving to remember the words and pick up his cues, such accidents for someone like George could not be avoided. On the Friday evening he was about to tumble head-over-heels using this piece of furniture as you might use a vaulting horse in a gymnasium, but recovered just in time. Noël Coward is one of many in show business who are credited with describing the art of acting as: 'Speak clearly and don't bump into the furniture'. George had probably never heard of this expression but in any case some 'bumping into' did take place.

When he was to blame for periods of silence on stage, or there was a minor collision with one of the other actors, the audience were generous in their tolerance although they could not resist a laugh arising from an incident not of Mr Coward's fashioning.

I absolutely refuse to change all our plans at the last moment, just because you think you've seen Elyot. It's unreasonable and ridiculous of you to demand it. Even if he is here I can't see that it matters. He'll probably feel much more embarrassed than you, and a damn good job too; and if he annoys you in any way I'll knock him down.

George delivered the speech perfectly, and with the right measure of scorn, but could not resist, at the end of the lines, squaring up to Amanda like a lethargic Joe Louis and swinging his fist through the air. Ruth was somewhat put off but delivered the next line in an even more scathing manner than she might have done with the original Victor.

That would be charming.

Without blaming Eric, there were naturally some backstage lapses; it would not be amateur dramatics if there was not the occasional clanger. On the second night, Simon managed to drop one of the plant pots used in Act One. He did this with such a resounding success that the audience, not at the bar and still in their seats during the interval, vigorously applauded the shattering sound that emanated from behind the closed curtains. Ambrose was rather angry.

I think it was on the same night, or possibly the third, that during Act Three Amanda is serving coffee and holding up the coffee pot and milk jug, smiles sweetly at Sibyl and says:

Half and half?

Simple enough except the props lady had omitted to include a milk jug. Ruth did not blink an eyelid and showed the coffee pot to Sibyl and said, 'Black I presume?'

For some reason Adrian had fallen in love with *Some Enchanted Evening* and for the music played in the interval he simply repeated the same tune, time after time – until Ambrose stormed backstage and battered the young man's head with a copy of the fat programme and said he never wanted to hear that particular piece of music again for the rest of his natural. This music man also contributed to the occasional lapse in concentration by the efficient prompter. When he was not required to be pressing buttons he would appear behind my chair and blow gently at the nape of my neck. Very disturbing.

The efficacy of the sound effects may have been fragile, but the lighting was a resounding success. Sam created just the atmosphere Ambrose had sought throughout the rehearsal process and there is no doubt, in Act One, the gradual fall of twilight enhanced the marvellous exchange between Elyot and Amanda as they moved inexorably towards their joint flight.

ELYOT:You're looking very lovely you know, in this damned moonlight. Your skin is clear and cool, and your eyes are shining, and you're growing lovelier and lovelier every second as I look at you. You don't hold any mystery for me, darling, do you mind? There isn't a particle of you that I don't know, remember, and want.
AMANDA [softly]: I'm glad, my sweet.
ELYOT:More than any desire anywhere, deep down in my deepest heart I want you back again – please –
AMANDA [putting her hand over his mouth]:Don't say any more; you're making me cry so dreadfully.

And so, the final curtain came down. All's well that ends well. A major disaster was avoided, mainly thanks to Helen, but perhaps her intervention will lead, indirectly, to a changed organisation – the Players under a different guise? If the Scotland's absence becomes a regular feature, there will be more opportunities for new stars: and have we seen the emergence of two of these with the performances

145

of Ruth and Alison? Has Miss Twining benefited from her involvement? Is there to be a new Chairman?

Our usual last night party follows a very traditional pattern, varied only as to numbers. The extent of the backstage staff is fairly constant but different plays feature a variable number of characters so the party attendees can fluctuate, but not by many. Supporters of the society who are in the last night audience often stay afterwards and join the celebrations together with the spouses and boy and girl friends of those involved in the performance. The party begins its life at the bar in the foyer but as drinks are acquired there is a drift into the Hall proper where the stage staff have stacked most of the chairs at the rear and provided a trestle table or two where the food we have brought to soak up the alcohol can be displayed.

As I have already told you, more than once, the throng are treated to the Chairman's speech, the prelude to a presentation of a gift to the Director of the day as a token of the Society's gratitude for his, or her, labours. It is always the same gift; a pewter tankard with the name of the show and the date engraved thereon. Providing same is of course one of my duties. We no longer fill the mug with ale and insist the recipient swallow the lot in one gulp; well, not since Ambrose brought up the contents in a warm stream of puke over the elegant two-piece in which our dear Chairman's wife was clad. I think that was the one where they lost Miss Prism's handbag and Ambrose had already sought relief in a number of backstage glasses of whisky.

However, for *Private Lives* there was a change of programme. Trevor had not been so informed but Ambrose was in the secret and before our Chairman could begin to utter his familiar words, the brilliant Director called for order by banged an empty beer bottle on one of the trestle tables, causing some insipid sausage rolls to perform an elaborate ballet on their paper plate.

"Boys and girls. One and all. Before our Chairman takes centre stage we have, for one night only, a novelty item. Would you all look towards the stage and, might I say, our triumphant stage and as you will see one of the settees has been placed in the centre of the hall where it will become the loci for an entertainment written and to be performed by our dear Vera and Mr Owen Ready. They have called this little divertissement *A Cavalcade of Coward*."

146

This was said with such gusto that we all began to clap wildly, whether in anticipation of what was to come or because we welcomed anything that delayed Trevor's monologue.

As the applause died down, Vera appeared wearing a shiny long dress with a white fox fur over her shoulders and a sparkling tiara adorning her shingled hair. She smiled at us all as Owen entered resplendent in the uniform of an officer of Her Majesty's Royal Navy.

Claude, are you leaving me soon? Portsmouth, I presume.

Darling Rosamund. Yes. In which we serve.

Oh, for moonlight and roses.

After we have dealt with the Hun.

Someday I'll find you.

I trust so.

Have you packed your silk dressing gown?

Yes, my precious.

And your silken drawers?

Could not do without them.

Write to me, won't you.

Of course.

Will your wife be at the quay to kiss you goodbye?

I suppose so.

Wonderful women. Please try not to push her off the dock.

Of course. When is Reginald coming for you?

Oh, he's already here. In the pink room.

You mean when I was making passionate love to you he was only next-door?

Yes. With another woman. Your mother. He's madly in love with her.

Extraordinary. Where does that leave you?

I shall wait for you my dearest, but should you be lost at sea the Earl of Brancaster has promised to step into the breach and I shall become mad about the boy.

Sloppy Branny. Never. I shall go AWOL.

They then joined hands and swung their arms together while singing a refrain from *Sail Away*.

When you can't bear the clamour of the noisy town,
Sail away – sail away.
When the friend that you counted on has let you down,
Sail away – sail away.
But when, soon or late,
You recognize your fate,
That will be your great, great day.
On the wings of the morning with your own true love,
Sail away – sail away.

At this, consummate performers that they are, Vera and Owen quickly stripped off their upper class skins and under gown and uniform we see Vera is wearing a pinafore with lisle stockings rolled down around her ankles, while Owen is in shirt sleeves, no collar or tie and braces hanging down to his heels. The dialogue is presented in the broadest of cockney accents.

Mother. What you got for me tea.
Kippers.

This response brought a smile to those of us who remembered *Spring and. Port Wine*. Even Ambrose tittered.

Not again. Why can't we have faggots? Me Mam always had faggots on a Saturday before she went down to the Bricklayers Arms.
Well, you can go back to your Mam.
Oh dear, don't be cross. Let's have a dance.
All right then. Give us a kiss.

Adrian surpassed himself as the two marvellous old troupers danced to a medley that contained *Poor Little Rich Girl* and *Mad About The Boy*.

Where's our Ida?
Out with that butcher's lad,
Not much by way of prospects there then.

Well, no more than thee. You were only a telegraph boy when I was daft enough to get wed.

Right. But we ain't done so badly.

Sure. We is what they call the salt of the earth.

That's as maybe, but I could do with some chips to put that salt on, together with the kipper you promised me.

Sorry love. Think the cat got it.

As a finale, Owen added a black top hat to his ensemble while Vera donned a battered straw that I recognized as that used by the Scarecrow in the *Wizard of Oz*. So equipped, they sang, alternating every two lines, a refrain from the Master's song, *I went to a marvellous party*, plus another of their own devising. From the original they could have chosen one of five refrains, they are all equally witty, but they selected the one about Baba and a turtle.

> I went to a marvellous party,
> We didn't start dinner till ten.
> And young Bobbie Carr
> Did a stunt at the bar
> With a lot of extraordinary men.
> Dear Baba arrived with a turtle.
> Which shattered us all to the core,
> The grand Duke was dancing a foxtrot with me
> When suddenly Cyril screamed Fiddledidee
> And ripped off his trousers and jumped in the sea,
> I couldn't have liked it more.

The words of their own making, a genuine joint effort Vera told me afterwards, were, I thought, a creditable pastiche. She gave me a copy.

> I went to the after-show party,
> Ambrose has triumphed again.
> We all loved Amanda,
> And will try to save her
> From Norfolk, the Fens and the rain.
> The fight scenes couldn't be bettered,

> The girls gave as good as they got.
> And Elyot singing *A Room with a View*
> Was all so surprising and terribly new.
> We hope that the Master is not going to sue,
> I couldn't have liked it more.

After that, even Trevor saw little point in producing his well-worn speech. He whispered something to his wife, that made her squirm a little, and then in a very few words thanked Ambrose and all the members for a fabulous show, whereupon Dot moved forward and kissed our Director on his forehead before presenting the usual pewter pot. This unprecedented action rendered dear Ambrose speechless and so George, amazingly, took the initiative and called for the three cheers for the Players and a hearty round of applause for the contribution by Vera and Owen.

If we thought their act was unique, it was as nothing to when Owen began to hand round glasses of champagne, donated, he told us all, by a benefactor who wished to remain anonymous. As you can imagine, I was intrigued. Could it possibly be a peace offering from the Scotland's? Not very likely, I thought, but such a gesture was no more incredulous than the true story that became public, to me, a few days later. This largesse had come from the Chairman. Can you believe it? Did he feel threatened? Was this a first step in a campaign designed to appoint him as Chairman for life?

I have not yet told you that I have a high level of tolerance to the effects of alcohol. No doubt inherited from my mother, but the addition of champagne stretched that tolerance to the point that by the end of the evening I was conscious of the fact that it would be unwise to attempt to drive myself home; and, in my view, Adrian was even more incapable of being safe while in charge of a motor vehicle. By the time of this realisation most everyone had left. Dot and Trev rarely stay late and normally Iris removed Ambrose from the scene at a reasonable hour to allow for the release of the babysitter they employ for their youngest, but on this night of all nights, some licence had been allowed and I could see that the bubbly was visibly heightening his pleasure at this momentous occasion. Even so, as I looked around the assorted company I could see that Ruth had left with George and Helen and I was there with only Eric and the usual scattering of back stage folk, always the last to leave, plus our Elyot and Sibyl. As I thought about asking Eric for transport back to my lonely bed, Jeremy, who had been discussing cricket with Adrian for what seemed to be the last hour and a half, came over to Alison and me and suggested we had a final drink at his house, from where both of us could walk home.

To say I was surprised understates the case; but perhaps it was again the champagne that accounted for this uncharacteristic invitation. Alison accepted on behalf of us all and the next thing I knew I was holding hands with Adrian while reclining on the plush leather-clad rear seats of Jeremy's light blue Jaguar. Rather different from the rear compartment of a Morris Minor. I had, of course, never been to his house before and as we entered the sitting room I naturally thought of Ruth. Nevertheless, it hardly looked like the arena of a seducer; in fact, it was warm, nicely furnished and most welcoming.

Our host decided that brandy should be the tipple of choice and I could not argue with that, although I did object when the two men attempted to ignore Alison and me as they tried to choose the England team for the forthcoming trip to New Zealand. I succeeded in halting their boring duologue by attempting a few lines of Coward's, *I went to a marvellous party*, whereupon Alison surprised us all by rising to her feet and insisting Adrian should dance with her while she sang, *Someday I'll Find You*. Astonishingly, she was word perfect, even if slightly out of tune but as to the dancing, I think she needed Adrian's close support to remain upright.

Jeremy sat back and beamed at all of us – and I think he winked at me as he left the room to find another bottle and open a tin of olives, the ones that are stuffed with anchovies. And then, can you believe it, he pressed a button on some huge music-making machine standing in the corner of the room and then took me in his arms and we danced most daintily across the Axminster with his cheek next to mine. By this time Adrian was fast asleep and there were signs that Alison might follow suit shortly so our host suggested we should ignore the recumbent newspaperman and he would walk the ladies to their doors, which he did. Alison first, whereupon she gave him a delicate kiss of thanks, as did I when we reached my abode.

It was of course a Saturday night, or rather a Sunday morning, and my mother, with my approval, had not foregone her regular visit to the Bell to be at the last-night party and so, as I tiptoed upstairs, I could hear a rhythmical snoring emanating from her bedroom. I welcomed the cool sheets in mine as I wondered whether I had misjudged Mr Jeremy Coxon from the start, or was it just the alcohol? I dreamt about him – at least I think I did.

At the outset of my tale, I wondered if it was right and proper to refer to our Chairman and the now triumphant Director as a pair of comedians akin to Morecambe and Wise or Laurel and Hardy. Comics, particularly those who operate within the framework of a clown, are used to being knocked down and then getting up either joyful or grumpy. Within that definition, Ambrose clearly qualifies. There can have been few acts of being 'knocked down' to equal the defection of one quarter of the acting ensemble just before the play was due to be staged, but he bounced back with a smile on his face and a twinkle in his eye. Trev is so little involved in the actual play production he does not need to exhibit any reaction to such disasters, but it certainly amused me when he began to realise that some counter attack was required to see off a possible competition for the position of Chairman. He must have heard of the accolades being heaped on Helen for rescuing this production.

Of course, this is of little consequence. The next AGM is over nine months away and my concern is not to begin planning Helen's campaign but to get to the bottom of the mystery of the Scotlands. I still did not believe Roger gave up the chance to triumph as Elyot because Ambrose insulted him: no doubt there are plenty of temperamental folk involved in our group, but not that unbalanced.

Our *Private Lives* may have provided Ruth with her Mr Right and possibly added something to the character of that shy and reticent May Twining. Has she found romance with that louche newspaper boy or is she too concerned with the private lives of Roger and Brenda Scotland to concentrate on her own? Allied to these concerns, are we to lose our convenient town-centre travel agency and if so, who will arrange honeymoon trips for Ruth and me to Paris – or Great Yarmouth?

Chapter Nine

Afterword

AFTER THE excitement of *Private Lives* I insisted Ambrose took a break and we spent five days in the Lake District. It was cold, but fortunately little rain fell and we were able to enjoy one or two healthy walks as well as the delight of drinking too much wine. We went to the cinema in Kendal – a rare treat for us as we do not have one at home – where they were showing a season of old hits; and guess what we saw, *Brief Encounter*. We both cried most of the way through. What a talent Mr Coward had. The hotel was virtually empty and so we were well looked after; it did him a power of good, and I enjoyed it as well.

I was proud of Ambrose and the way he managed to rescue *Private Lives* from the brink of disaster. Of course, if it had not been for Helen this would not have been possible but with George stepping into the breach, my clever husband still had to work very hard. The final effort was not as polished as it would have been with Roger included but I doubt if too many in the audience realised this and everyone I have spoken to enjoyed it.

For posterity's sake, should posterity care, we have a commentary on this production from May who has written a history, from her point of view, but I believe it would be helpful if, as an informed outsider – I did nothing except support Ambrose – I provide an Afterword, a postscript as it were, that the imaginative Miss Twining can add to her idiosyncratic ramblings if she so wishes. She has given me a copy of her account, which is a relatively amusing mixture of truth and whimsy, but what must be noted is the fact that she is involved in an Open University course on Creative Writing which might explain some of her more extreme flights of fancy.

In her story of this Coward extravaganza it is Mr Scotland who emerges as the rogue, or at least the number one enigma, and I suppose that is the case. We told May about the supermarket problem but as that matter progressed it was clear that firstly, the developer was not going to proceed and secondly, Roger was not as involved as we first thought. May exaggerates our concern over this for the sake of dramatic tension; it can be seen as what Alfred Hitchcock would call 'the MacGuffin'. This began with the suggestion that there was something shady involved in the development at Holmfield Farm followed up by a picture of Roger as the arch-villain cum agent acting for a property developer and where he is ready to cast aside a long friendship with Ambrose and me for the sake of the filthy lucre. We were approached to see if we would sell the shop, but we said no and that was that. References to Rosa Luxemburg and Karl Marx are the product of an over-wrought imagination because the real clue is of course the Investment Club.

The eventual hiatus he caused was, on the surface, really Ambrose's fault with his careless, even thoughtless, remarks at the pre-Dress Rehearsal, although he denies using the word 'ham' and I believe him. He is too experienced for that but we all thought Roger would not have given up the chance to play Elyot Chase just because Ambrose expressed some dissatisfaction at such a late stage in the rehearsal process. There had to be another reason, and there was, as I shall reveal.

But before then, some less important points which I have arranged, more or less sequentially, following May's writing. Firstly, Trevor Jointing. Not a very flattering portrait is it, and she knows very well that before moving to Great Selsdon he sold the family business, a chain of shoe shops throughout the Midlands, to the British Shoe Corporation. He and Dorothy worked hard building up this operation and they were both pleased at the sale which allowed them to retire in comfort. I suppose he is a trifle pompous but he is not a misogynist and Ambrose thinks he is a good Chairman although if ever Helen wants to take over, and May makes great play over this, I am sure Trevor will be delighted, as has proved to be the case. Our cleric does marginally stutter but as for him being the leader of a coup to unseat the present incumbent, just a minor piece of embroidery.

Next, I wish to deal with my dear Ambrose as a Lothario. Depends on your interpretation of the word. He is what might be called a ladies man; he enjoys their company but has never had any designs or desire to progress to a stage beyond a smile and a holding of hands. He knows I would not tolerate more than this but, of course, May's description adds something extra to her account – although I think she does eventually acknowledge that Alison was chosen simply because Ambrose saw the potential in the girl and not just as a result of her brilliant blue eyes. And how right he was: I thought she excelled.

My husband was mildly irritated by May's description of the Pottinger taglines and he was not over-enthusiastic about her poetic ability. I rather like the rhyming of 'smaller' with 'trawler' but both of us thought she was way off the mark using social class to describe a difference between us and the Scotlands. Totally wrong; none of us would see any trace of that in our relationship.

He is by no means as frequent a Director as is alleged. The farrago about choosing a play is, so Ambrose assures me, exactly that. No one wants to be the Director and so when there is a volunteer prepared to take on the task they invariably do so with a play in mind. It is of course common knowledge that both Rattigan and Coward were homosexuals – May has some minor fun over this – but she omits to inform you that our Postmaster is also of that persuasion, and rather more intelligent than she describes.

I discussed with Ambrose May's view that continued involvement in amateur theatre is addictive and that sometimes actors can become so wrapped up in what they are doing they take on, for a time, the personality of the character they play. He agrees that this does happen, but only rarely. James Roderick, the headmaster who was in *Educating Rita*, had the reputation of being something of a drinker before being exposed to Willy Russell, but whether his affection for the bottle got more intense, I cannot say. What is clear is that Roger has a very stable persona, generally, and any changes in his character are most unlikely to be influenced by a stage role.

But, what about the character of our chronicler? Ambrose is well aware that despite her genuine interest in the theatre, she does suffer from a virulent strain of the disease of stage fright. He also confirms that she can be a valuable lieutenant to any Director but I suspect she exaggerates her bust size.

Her portraits of Vera and Owen are accurate, to an extent, but why she needed to suggest that Vera is a reformed alcoholic, I cannot imagine. This piece of fiction does not really add a great deal to the story but obviously May has tried to drive the vehicle of sensationalism as hard as possible, without being too incredible. The relationship between Jeremy and Ruth is one of fellow thespians, and nothing more, and George's display of the pugilist's art is pure fantasy. Jackson is not exactly a ball of fire and Ambrose thinks we really should appoint a more energetic Treasurer, but as to him having any romantic inclination towards his fellow Committee member, not a chance. Mavis would have him consigned to the medieval stocks that still grace the Market Place and pelted with rotten eggs.

Ambrose and I thought May's invention about a proposal to set the play in Norfolk was brilliant. Added a really amusing twist. She also did well describing the show put on by Vera and Owen at the after-play party, even though she omits to record that both Trevor and Ambrose encouraged and supported this when Owen made the suggestion that a pastiche of Coward would be a worthwhile project– and not too difficult

Where she likes the people we are given sympathetic portraits and these are justified in the case of Vera, Owen and Ruth, even though with Miss Thurston Brown there are hidden depths not apparent to our reporter. None of us know Jeremy too well, but by all accounts he is going to be a valuable member of the Society although I am sure May's estimate as to his age is somewhat adrift. I suspect we will also find that Alison is going to figure prominently in future productions where there is a part for an ingénue. If there is a bug, as May propounds, I wager Miss Street has been infected, She even talked to Ambrose about Ibsen's Nora but then, more realistically, said she would love to do Eliza Doolittle if the Players ever reprise *Pygmalion*.

The revelation I promised about Roger is, I am afraid, rather banal. May's flight of fancy about Brenda and a one-night stand with a young man called Rufus does contain one particle of truth when she tells of her husband's early years. He did come from a lowly background. His mother was left to bring him up when the father was fatally hit by a car outside a pub, premises where he was a regular visitor. Evidently the driver was not to blame – the dead man was so intoxicated he could hardly stand.

He and Brenda did meet in Bristol but, as it was in those days, I am ready to wager that the first time they slept together was on their honeymoon, which was not in Deauville, and the idea of James being conceived out of wedlock is nonsense

Roger had to work hard to qualify as a solicitor and find a place in a much respected firm. Such experience often hardens a person, makes them more able than most to overcome obstacles along life's way and it is perhaps this that has contributed to the hauteur that May dwells upon – over much in my view. On the other hand, without the benefit of a stable upbringing perhaps temptations are more difficult to resist and so, by the time Roger had struggled on and become a well-remunerated partner in Rogers and Co, he could not resist the prospect of further riches being acquired, not by hard work, but by gambling.

I cannot comment on why this fever should have affected a man like Roger, but it did. Initially Brenda was unaware of what was happening but as the losses grew, she inevitably discovered what her husband was doing. At the time of *Private Lives* their savings were being dissipated at an alarming rate and this was beginning to affect their relationship with each other. In fashion, with addicts of this pernicious fever, Roger promised to give up but succumbed to temptation with the classic excuse that one last flutter would retrieve all previous losses.

Just before *Private Lives* opened, Brenda had threatened to leave him when the ownership of their house was put into jeopardy and this so disturbed him that he was pushed into that piece of irrationality – walking out on Ambrose. He did not go so far as to kiss Alison before he left the stage but Brenda told me later that his insistence that she desert with him was the turning point. He loves acting and the trauma of his action in giving up Elyot at the last minute was the medicine he needed. The possible loss of his house, and his family, was not enough but his traitorous behaviour towards the Players – as he subsequently described it – was the last straw. The fact that deserting a theatre group was, at that moment, more disastrous than losing his wife seems as far-fetched as some of May's more extreme imaginings, but that is what happened. Incredible as it might seem, *Private Lives* restored Roger back to a solid citizen – and also, as I shall detail, brought romance to Miss Twining.

Despite May's attempts to show that a number of people's future lives were affected by this production, it seems that the greatest impact was felt by the Players as an organisation rather than changing any particular individual. May surmised that the status of Helen within the Group would be enhanced as a result of her intervention at the time of Roger's desertion, and this came to be. Trevor himself negotiated her appointment to the Committee with the fullest intention that she is to be his heir apparent, but of even more importance was the waning of the Scotland star and the rising of those of Ruth and Jeremy – and Alison I suppose. Waning is too strong a word. Once Roger had the family's financial situation under control, he and Brenda continued to display their undoubted talents, in competition with the newer stars, but without the automatic assumption that they would be awarded the best parts.

I am not acquainted with the detail, but I understand Roger resigned from the partnership and extinguished all of his gambling debts with the capital he withdrew from the firm. They were able to stay at Holmfield Farm and the pension fund he had accumulated while working enabled them to live relatively comfortably – and he did manage to get a novel published, which is more than can be said for May.

In addition, with more free time on his hands, he volunteered to take on the job of Director and offered to entertain the good folk of Great Selsdon with a production of *Medea,* but I think more likely it will be *Pygmalion* again, giving Ambrose a chance to do Higgins alongside his protégé as Eliza. A fitting prospect: the Svengali in the real world of *Private Lives* reprises his role as the fictional Professor. Brenda told me that in the same mood as a move to Norfolk was mooted for the Coward play, Roger is thinking of casting Ruth as Colonel Pickering.

Even more surprising is the rumour currently circulating amongst the Players, and not I am assured initiated by May, that Brenda and Vera are really planning a joint production of *Oliver* for next Christmas, provided they can find the necessary juniors who can sing. The adult roles open up a fascinating permutation of candidates and I believe they have already pencilled in Roger or Jeremy as Bill Sykes, Owen as Fagin and Alison as Nancy, even though she will need a lot of coaching for *As Long As He Needs Me*.

Ambrose and I have two wedding presents to buy; in the Spring Ruth is to be wed to a teacher colleague of hers, Malcolm Barton – he does Maths and Cricket so we are told – and May is to become Mrs Jeremy Coxon two weeks later. Roger is to be the best man and Ambrose has agreed to act as the father-of-the bride. There is nothing in her story that gives a hint that the forty-eight-year-old Jeremy might have been attracted to that young lady approaching thirty but, as the 1950s hit had it, *Love Is Strange*.

Tricia was heard to say that she was marrying him for his money, but that is not how May operates. Again, she does not tell you that during the *Private Lives* saga she was promoted to Assistant Branch Manager at the bank, in charge of Commercial Lending and she also fails to mention that she is halfway to becoming a Chartered Accountant, a fact much too boring for her quirky writings. They will be good for each other. Perhaps her next piece of fiction will be based on his African experiences.

Lightning Source UK Ltd.
Milton Keynes UK
10 December 2009

147335UK00001B/147/P